Books should be returned on or before the
last date stamped below

0 2 JUL 2011

1 4 SEP 2011

ABERDEENSHIRE
LIBRARIES

WITHDRAWN
FROM LIBRARY

ABERDEENSHIRE LIBRARY
AND INFORMATION SERVICE
MELDR Grant, Reg   M

The Vietnam War
/ Reg Grant

J959.
7
1561869

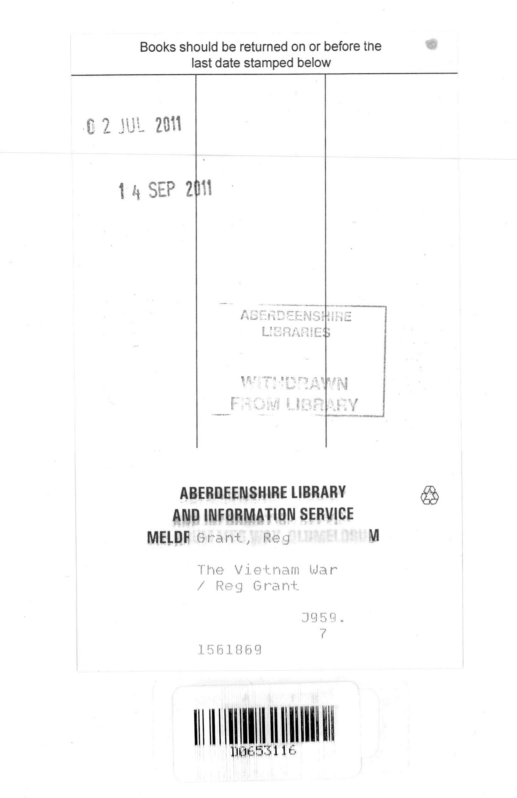

D0653116

THE VIETNAM WAR

Reg Grant

W

FRANKLIN WATTS

LONDON•SYDNEY

Titles in this series:

THE ARAB-ISRAELI CONFLICT
THE KOREAN WAR
THE VIETNAM WAR
WORLD WAR I
WORLD WAR II: EUROPE
WORLD WAR II: THE PACIFIC

© 2004 Arcturus Publishing

Produced for Franklin Watts by Arcturus Publishing Ltd, 26/27 Bickels Yard, 151-153 Bermondsey Street, London SE1 3HA.

Series concept: Alex Woolf
Editor: Philip de Ste. Croix
Designer: Simon Borrough
Cartography: The Map Studio
Consultant: Paul Cornish, Imperial War Museum, London
Picture researcher: Thomas Mitchell

Published in the UK by Franklin Watts.

All rights reserved. No part of this publication may be reproduced, stored in a retrieval system, or transmitted, in any form or by any means without the prior written permission of the publisher, nor be otherwise circulated in any form of binding or cover other than that in which it is published and without a similar condition being imposed on the subsequent purchaser.

A CIP catalogue record for this book is available from the British Library.

ISBN 0 7496 5450 3

Printed and bound in Italy

Franklin Watts – the Watts Publishing Group, 96 Leonard Street, London EC2A 4XD.

Picture Acknowledgements:
All the photographs in this book, with the exception of those listed below, were supplied by Getty Images and are reproduced here with their permission.
Camera Press: page 41, page 50.
Popperfoto: page 46, page 47.

ABOUT THE AUTHOR

The author, Reg Grant, studied history at the University of Oxford, and is the author of more than a dozen books on modern history. He specializes in the history of the twentieth century. His book *The Holocaust* (1997) was shortlisted for the *Times Educational Supplement*'s Senior Information Book Award.

Grant, Reg

The Vietnam War
/ Reg Grant

                    J959.
                       7
1561869

CONTENTS

1. THE FIRST INDO-CHINA WAR   4

2. THE US IS SUCKED IN   10

3. SEARCH AND DESTROY
 – 1965-1967   18

4. THE DECISIVE YEAR – 1968   26

5. VIETNAMIZATION – 1969-1971   32

6. EASTER OFFENSIVE TO
 CHRISTMAS BOMBING   38

7. COMMUNISM TRIUMPHANT   44

8. AFTERMATH   48

PROFILES OF MILITARY
AND POLITICAL LEADERS   52

STATISTICS CONCERNING
COMBATANT NATIONS   55

SIGNIFICANT DATES   56

GLOSSARY   58

FURTHER INFORMATION   60

INDEX   62

CHAPTER 1:
THE FIRST INDO-CHINA WAR

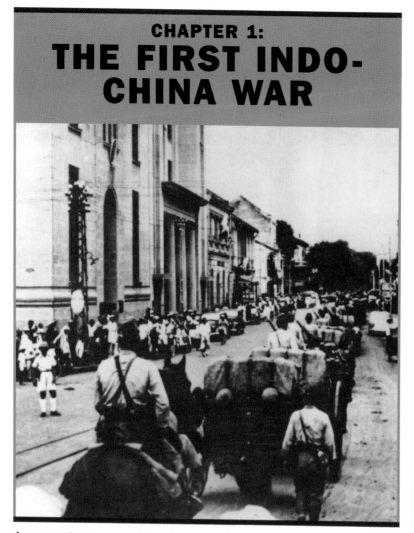

Japanese troops move into Vietnam in July 1941, beginning their four-year occupation of the country. Vietnam was at that time part of the colony of French Indo-China.

Vietnam is a country in south-east Asia with a population of about 80 million. Its recorded history stretches back more than 2,000 years. In the second half of the nineteenth century, at a time when European countries were extending their rule over much of Asia and Africa, it was conquered by the French. It became part of the colony of French Indo-China, along with its neighbours Cambodia and Laos.

From the start French rule was opposed by Vietnamese nationalists, but all opposition was harshly repressed by the French colonial authorities. In the early decades of the twentieth century, many nationalists took refuge abroad. They included Ho Chi Minh, the son of a Vietnamese official. In 1920, living in France, Ho became a communist. From then on, his life was dedicated to the two goals of achieving national independence for Vietnam and establishing a communist society in which private ownership of industry and land would be abolished.

The French remained firmly in control of Indo-China until the start of World War II (1939-45). Early in that war, in Europe, France was defeated by Germany. As a result, France was in no position to aid its colonists in Indo-China when they came under pressure from the rising power in Asia: Japan. In 1941, the French colonial authorities were forced to allow Japanese troops to occupy Indo-China. Although they left the French officially in control, the Japanese effectively ran the colony.

In the same year, Ho Chi Minh and other Vietnamese nationalists founded a guerrilla organization to fight both the Japanese and the French. They called it the Vietnam Doc Lap Dong Minh Hoi (League for the Independence of Vietnam) –

NATIONALIST OR COMMUNIST?

Tran Ngoc Danh, a colleague of Viet Minh leader Ho Chi Minh, wrote:
'How many times in my life have I been asked: you who know Ho Chi Minh so well, can you say whether he is a nationalist or a communist? The answer is simple: Ho Chi Minh is both. For him, nationalism and communism, the end and the means, complement one another…'
[Quoted in *Historical Atlas of the Vietnam War*, Summers and Karnow]

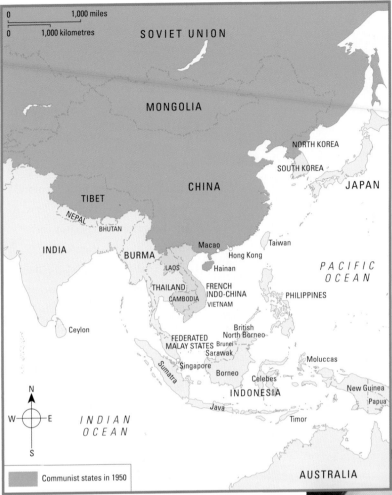

control of large areas of northern Vietnam. In March 1945, the Japanese abolished French rule in Indo-China, but the following August Japan surrendered to the United States and its allies. This left a power vacuum in Vietnam that the Viet Minh were quick to exploit. On 2 September 1945, in the northern city of Hanoi, Ho declared Vietnam independent under a Viet Minh government. In the southern city of Saigon, however, occupied by British troops, the French authorities were reinstalled in control.

At first there was a compromise. In March 1946 the Viet Minh and the French agreed that Vietnam would be a 'Free State' within the French Empire. But the following November

In the early 1950s, French Indo-China was on the edge of the communist-ruled area of Asia. America saw Indo-China as in the front line of its fight to halt the spread of communism.

or Viet Minh for short. The leaders of the Viet Minh were communists, including not only Ho but also the movement's chief military commander, Vo Nguyen Giap. But, as the name of the movement suggests, they appealed above all to the Vietnamese desire for national independence.

During World War II, the Viet Minh received support from the United States, which was itself at war with Japan from December 1941. Ho's guerrillas fought the Japanese with increasing success and won

General Vo Nguyen Giap commanded the Viet Minh forces during the First Indo-China War. This picture shows him later, as North Vietnamese Minister of Defence in 1966.

Viet Minh guerrillas cross an improvised bridge during their war against the French in 1953. Operating almost entirely on foot in Vietnam's rough terrain, the Viet Minh were formidable fighters.

fighting broke out between the French and the Viet Minh, first in the northern port city of Haiphong and then in Hanoi. The Viet Minh army withdrew from the cities to the countryside and launched a new guerrilla war against the French.

RED CHINA Until 1949 it seemed that the French would be able to contain the guerrillas. But in that year communists led by Mao Tse-tung won control of Vietnam's massive northern neighbour, China. Supplied with arms and equipment by the Chinese communists, the Viet Minh were able to take the initiative. With much of its territory mountainous and covered in thick jungle, Vietnam was ideal country for guerrillas to operate, hiding from and ambushing more heavily armed conventional troops. The French successfully defended the densely populated area of the Red River Delta in the north when the Viet Minh launched a major offensive in 1951, but isolated French outposts in rural areas were liable to be besieged and overrun.

France lacked the resources to sustain a war in Indo-China over a long period and soon became dependent on the support of the United States. In general, the US favoured independence for countries under European colonial rule. But from 1947 onwards, the United States was also committed to resisting the spread of

'ENDURING MEN...'

Major Marcel Bigeard, a French paratroop officer in Vietnam, expressed his admiration for the Viet Minh guerrillas: '*I can tell you they became the greatest infantry in the world: these enduring men capable of covering 50 kilometres in the night on the strength of a bowl of rice, with running shoes, and then singing their way into battle...*'

[Quoted in *Vietnam: The Ten Thousand Day War*, Michael Maclear]

communism, which was seen as a global threat to US interests. The communist triumph in China in 1949 made the US very worried about any possible further communist expansion in Asia. When communist North Korea invaded South Korea in 1950, American troops were sent in to resist the invasion. At the same time, American aid – money and arms – was provided to help the French fight the communist-led Viet Minh.

By the end of 1953 France's position in Vietnam was becoming desperate. The Viet Minh were not only growing in military strength but also had popular support among a people eager for independence from colonial rule. The French had set up a government under a traditional Vietnamese ruler, Emperor Bao Dai, but it attracted little support.

In an attempt to regain the military initiative, French commanders decided to establish a powerful base at Dien Bien Phu, a

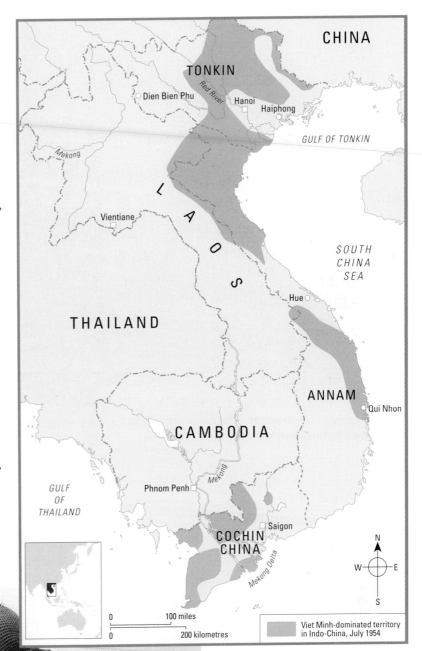

Under French rule, Vietnam was divided into three parts: Tonkin, Annam and Cochin China. In 1954 Viet Minh guerrillas dominated most of Tonkin outside the major cities, part of Annam and much of Cochin China.

A French doctor treats a Vietnamese soldier during the siege of Dien Bien Phu in 1954. Thousands of anti-communist Vietnamese fought alongside the French against the Viet Minh.

French paratroopers are dropped in to Dien Bien Phu. The base was shelled by Viet Minh artillery positioned in the mountains overlooking it.

remote site in northern Vietnam close to the border with Laos. They hoped the base would help block Viet Minh supply lines bringing men and arms into Vietnam, and prevent an expected Viet Minh attack on Laos. The Viet Minh saw an opportunity to inflict a decisive defeat on the colonial power. They assembled powerful infantry forces around Dien Bien Phu, hauling artillery up mountainsides overlooking the French positions, and in March 1954 they launched their attack. The French garrison, which consisted chiefly of elite parachute battalions, resisted fiercely. But they were surrounded and outnumbered, resupplied only by air.

France's only hope of avoiding a humiliating defeat lay in an appeal to the United States. In talks between senior French and American military commanders, a plan was devised for a massive aerial bombardment by US aircraft which would destroy the Viet Minh forces besieging Dien Bien Phu. US President Dwight D. Eisenhower, however, rejected involving American forces directly in support of the French.

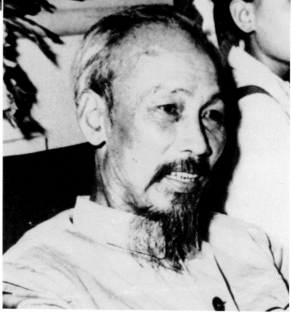

Vietnamese communist leader Ho Chi Minh was known as 'Uncle Ho', but he was ruthless in pursuit of his goal of a united, communist Vietnam.

DEFEAT AT DIEN BIEN PHU On 8 May 1954, the final French defences at Dien Bien Phu were overrun. On the same day, a peace conference opened in Geneva, Switzerland, to discuss an end to the war. The following July, a peace agreement, known as the Geneva Accords, gave Vietnam, Laos and Cambodia independence from France. But Vietnam was divided

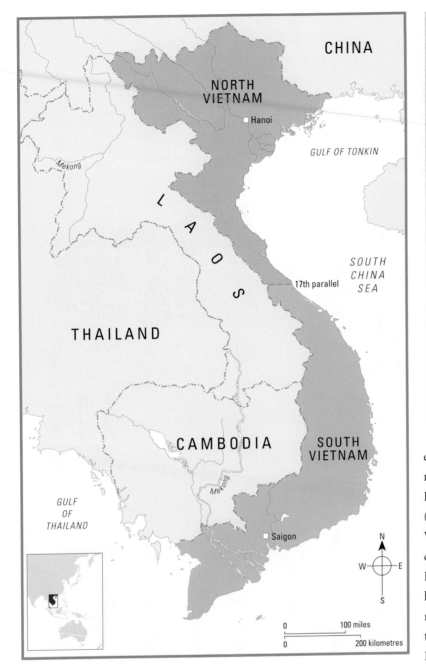

General Henri Navarre, the French commander in Indo-China at the time of the defeat at Dien Bien Phu, was critical of President Eisenhower's decision not to provide air support:

'There is no doubt that if the American air force had been heavily involved … Dien Bien Phu would certainly have been saved. The US would not have had to become involved later as it was obliged to do.'

[Quoted in *Vietnam: The Ten Thousand Day War*, Michael Maclear]

The Democratic Republic of Vietnam (North Vietnam) was separated from the Republic of Vietnam (South Vietnam) by a demilitarized zone (DMZ) along the 17th parallel.

in two, with Ho and the Viet Minh taking control north of the 17th parallel and Emperor Bao Dai ruling in the south.

According to the Geneva Accords, this division was supposed to be temporary. Vietnam was to be reunited in two years' time, after democratic elections to choose a government for the whole country. But no such elections were ever held. In the north, Ho established the Democratic Republic of Vietnam (usually referred to as North Vietnam), a state ruled by the communist Vietnamese Workers' Party. North Vietnam became a hardline communist state very much like those that then existed in the Soviet Union, China, North Korea, and Eastern Europe. In the south, Emperor Bao Dai was soon replaced as ruler of the Republic of Vietnam (South Vietnam) by Ngo Dinh Diem, a tough leader who had the backing of the United States.

After the Geneva Accords, about 900,000 Vietnamese, feeling there was no place for them in a communist state, chose to move from North Vietnam to the South. At the same time, some 100,000 Viet Minh fighters withdrew from South Vietnam to the North. The division of Vietnam was destined to last for more than twenty years.

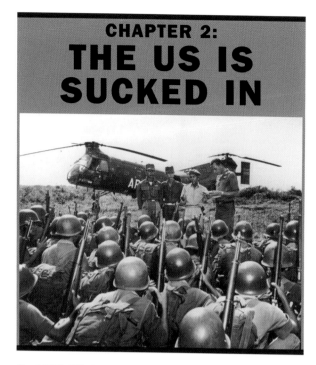

CHAPTER 2: THE US IS SUCKED IN

The United States regarded the French defeat in Indo-China and the establishment of a communist state in North Vietnam as a serious setback in its efforts to resist the spread of communism worldwide. The Americans were determined to prevent any further expansion of communist rule in South-east Asia. To this end, from 1954 onwards they undertook to support the state of South Vietnam, aiming to turn it into a stable country capable of defending itself against an attack from North Vietnam or internal subversion. In 1956 the United States set up a Military Assistance Advisory Group in the Southern capital, Saigon (it later became the Military Assistance Command Vietnam – MACV). US money, arms and military advisers were provided to build up an Army of the Republic of South Vietnam (ARVN).

The United States was well aware that the future of South Vietnam also depended on good government. Here problems quickly mounted. Ngo Dinh Diem belonged to the Catholic minority in Vietnam, and soon aroused the hostility of Vietnamese Buddhists.

By 1962, US Army officers were 'advising' South Vietnamese soldiers fighting communist-led guerrillas and US helicopter pilots were flying them into battle.

South Vietnamese President Ngo Dinh Diem visits New York in May 1957. At this time he enjoyed the full support of the United States, but the Americans later came to see him as a liability.

His regime was neither liberal nor democratic – opposition newspapers were closed down and the secret police, the Can Lao, was much feared. In rural South Vietnam, Diem failed to carry through a land reform which might have won over the peasants to his side. Instead, he raised taxes and replaced locally elected village leaders with his own appointed officials. Soon discontent was rife in the countryside. In 1957-8, isolated terrorist attacks began to occur, including the assassination of government officials.

In May 1959, the government of North Vietnam decided that the time was ripe to promote a guerrilla war in South Vietnam, with the aim of overthrowing Diem and reuniting Vietnam under communist rule. Thousands of experienced Viet Minh cadres (officers) were sent back from the North into South Vietnam with orders to begin building up a guerrilla movement in the countryside. Work began on organizing a supply route from the North to the South through Laos and Cambodia – a complex pattern of roads and tracks that became known as the Ho Chi Minh Trail. Arms and men were also carried into the South by sea, mainly by small boats sailing down to the Mekong Delta south of Saigon.

The southern guerrilla movement called itself the National Liberation Front (NLF), although to the US the guerrillas were always

Supplies from North Vietnam were carried to guerrillas in the South along jungle trails in Laos or Cambodia and by small boats along the coast. Much of the equipment originated in China.

DOMINO THEORY

One of the major justifications for America's support for South Vietnam lay in the 'domino theory' – the belief that if South Vietnam fell to communism many other countries in Asia would also fall like a line of dominoes. Senator (later President) John F. Kennedy stated in 1956: *'Burma, Thailand, India, Japan, the Philippines and obviously Laos and Cambodia are among those whose security would be threatened if the red tide of communism overflowed into Vietnam.'*

[Quoted in *America in Vietnam*, Guenter Lewy]

the Viet Cong (VC). The NLF was officially founded in 1960. It took care to appeal to Vietnamese nationalism, describing the guerrilla war as a continuation of the struggle previously fought against the French, with the Americans now as the 'imperialist' power.

The NLF swiftly built up a strong position in rural South Vietnam. Young men were recruited from the villages – sometimes voluntarily, sometimes not – and taken to remote areas for training as full-time members of the guerrilla army. They created the Viet Cong 'mainforce', capable of taking on the ARVN and, later, the Americans, in major operations. At the same time, many peasants who stayed in the villages constituted a 'part-time' aid to the guerrillas, not only providing intelligence and

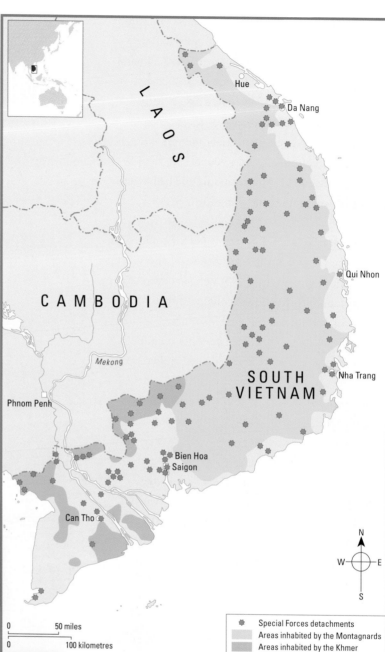

A US military adviser (second from left) looks on as an ARVN officer examines captured papers.

Jungle and mountain areas of South Vietnam were inhabited by people who were not ethnic Vietnamese. US Special Forces were able to organize many of them for anti-communist activity.

Map legend:
- Special Forces detachments
- Areas inhabited by the Montagnards
- Areas inhabited by the Khmer

| | 0 — 50 miles |
| | 0 — 100 kilometres |

US TROOPS IN SOUTH VIETNAM
The US military commitment to South Vietnam rose steeply between 1960 and 1964.

	1960	1961	1962	1963	1964
US military personnel	875	3,164	11,326	16,263	23,310
US deaths in action	0	1	31	77	137

food supplies, but also planting booby-trap bombs or taking part in ambushes of military patrols.

The first US casualties in Vietnam were military advisers wounded in a Viet Cong raid at Bien Hoa in July 1959. The following January an ARVN force was defeated by guerrillas north-east of Saigon. The US responded by increasing its force of military advisers in South Vietnam, from around 1,000 in 1960 to over 11,000, by the end of 1962, including 300 helicopter pilots who went into battle alongside the ARVN.

SPECIAL FORCES Strategies for counter-insurgency – that is, for defeating guerrilla movements – were a hot topic at this time. America's new president in 1961, John F. Kennedy, was convinced that wars against communist-led 'national liberation movements' were going to be crucial in the future. Kennedy was a keen advocate of the Green Berets, US Special Force troops who were trained in unconventional warfare techniques. From 1962, the Green Berets were sent in to organize resistance to the Viet Cong guerrillas among the Montagnard tribespeople – non-Vietnamese who lived in remote mountainous areas of Vietnam. The Montagnard Civilian Irregular Defense Groups (CIDGs) led and armed by the Green Berets operated with some success within Viet Cong-dominated areas. But their effect on the war was in the end only marginal.

Potentially a more effective form of counter-insurgency was the Strategic Hamlets programme, which also got under way in 1962. This involved shifting South Vietnamese peasants from their villages into large fortified settlements, where they could be defended from coercion by the guerrillas and, in theory, won over to the government side. In practice, however, nothing was done to win the 'hearts and minds' of the rural population. The Strategic Hamlets were little better than concentration camps and being herded into them only made the peasants more hostile to the South Vietnamese government.

Another programme begun at this time was the spraying of chemical defoliants from the air to destroy crops being grown to feed the Viet Cong and to clear areas of vegetation that might be used by the guerrillas

US Air Force planes loaded with chemical defoliants fly on a mission to spray an area of South Vietnamese forest where guerrillas were active.

A Buddhist monk burns himself to death in the street in protest at the policies of President Diem. The majority of South Vietnamese were Buddhists, but Diem was a Catholic.

GULF OF TONKIN RESOLUTION

The resolution passed by the US Congress on 7 August 1964, in the wake of the Gulf of Tonkin incident, denounced the alleged attacks on US warships as *'part of a deliberate and systematic campaign of aggression that the Communist regime in North Vietnam has been waging …'* and declared *'… that the Congress approve and support the determination of the President, as Commander in Chief, to take all necessary measures to repel any armed attack against the forces of the United States and to prevent further aggression.'*

as cover. Defoliant spraying was to expand into a large-scale – and highly controversial – operation, but it had little immediate effect in restricting guerrilla activity.

By 1963 the Viet Cong were in effective control of a large and expanding area of the South Vietnamese countryside. At the same time, Diem's position as the country's leader was collapsing. His rule had grown increasingly dictatorial and incompetent. Vietnamese Buddhists were in open conflict with the Diem regime. The American public was shocked by images of Buddhist monks burning themselves to death in the streets as a protest against Diem's rule.

In the autumn of 1963, the US government secretly gave the go-ahead to a group of South Vietnamese generals, led by General Duong Van Minh, who were plotting a military coup. On 1 November Diem was arrested and shot dead, along with his brother Nhu. Within three weeks of Diem's death, John F. Kennedy was shot and killed in Dallas, Texas, and replaced as US president by Lyndon B. Johnson. The new president confirmed the policy of supporting South Vietnam against what the United States termed 'communist aggression'.

General Minh and his colleagues proved even less capable than Diem of creating a stable government in Saigon that might win the war against the guerrillas. They soon

President Lyndon B. Johnson (seated) calls on the US Congress to support military action in Vietnam after the Gulf of Tonkin incident.

The attack or (disputedly) attacks on the USS *Maddox* by North Vietnamese torpedo boats led to retaliatory air strikes launched from US aircraft carriers.

squabbled bitterly among themselves and coup followed coup. In March 1964 US Secretary of Defense Robert McNamara visited Saigon to assess the situation. He concluded that South Vietnam was on the verge of total collapse. The US either had to admit defeat and allow Saigon to fall to the communists or increase its military involvement in the war.

The number of US military advisers in South Vietnam was consequently increased to 23,000 and General William C. Westmoreland was sent to head the MACV. But McNamara believed the war against the guerrillas in the South could only be a holding operation – buying time. The only way to save South Vietnam would be to persuade, or force, the North Vietnamese government to call a halt to the fighting.

NO INVASION The United States believed an invasion of North Vietnam was out of the question, as it would have led the Chinese to send in troops – as they had when North Korea was invaded by US-led forces in 1950. But US covert operations in North Vietnam and Laos had been taking place since 1961, and in January 1964 President Johnson secretly authorized hit-and-run raids by gunboats along the North Vietnamese coast.

US warships were sometimes sent to patrol the Gulf of Tonkin, off the coast of North Vietnam, in support of these secret raids. On 2 August 1964, the American destroyer USS *Maddox* was sailing about 16 km off the North Vietnamese coast when it was attacked by North Vietnamese torpedo boats. The boats were driven off with the aid of aircraft from the carrier USS *Ticonderoga*. President Johnson announced that any further 'unprovoked military action' by North Vietnam would lead to 'grave consequences'.

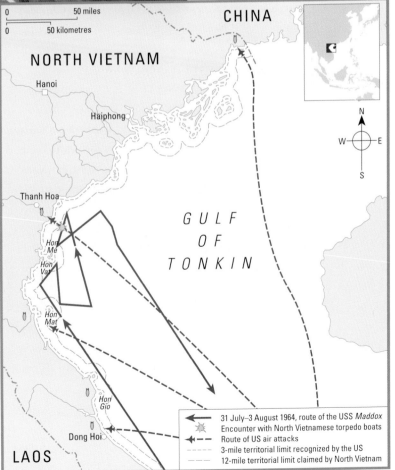

0 — 50 miles	
0 — 50 kilometres	

CHINA

NORTH VIETNAM

Hanoi

Haiphong

Thanh Hoa

Hon Me

Hon Vat

GULF OF TONKIN

Hon Mat

Hon Gio

Dong Hoi

LAOS

N
W — E
S

← 31 July–3 August 1964, route of the USS *Maddox*
✳ Encounter with North Vietnamese torpedo boats
◄--- Route of US air attacks
----- 3-mile territorial limit recognized by the US
----- 12-mile territorial limit claimed by North Vietnam

Two days later, on the night of 4-5 August, *Maddox* and another destroyer reported that they had once again been attacked by enemy vessels. It has been widely questioned whether this second attack actually took place. However, President Johnson ordered immediate air strikes in retaliation, and aircraft from the carriers *Ticonderoga* and *Constellation* bombarded North Vietnamese ports. On 7 August, the US Congress passed what is known as the Gulf of Tonkin Resolution, which in effect gave the US government a free hand to escalate US involvement in Vietnam in any way it saw fit.

ROLLING THUNDER STATISTICS

The Rolling Thunder bombing campaign against North Vietnam in 1965-8 was on a massive scale:

Sorties flown by US Navy and Air Force fighter bombers	304,000
Sorties by B-52 bombers over North Vietnam	2,380
Bombs dropped (tons)	537,000
US aircraft lost in combat	922

ROLLING THUNDER
The next US bombing raids on North Vietnam followed in February 1965, in retaliation for guerrilla attacks on US bases in South Vietnam. Then, on 2 March 1965, the United States initiated a sustained bombing campaign against the North. Known as Operation Rolling Thunder, this campaign continued, with a number of interruptions, until October 1968.

The aim of Rolling Thunder was to persuade North Vietnam to call off the fight in the South. The bombing raids were carefully graded, with attacks periodically stepped up or reduced as a way of bullying or coaxing the North Vietnamese into stopping the war. Many targets were permanently off-limits – mostly to avoid provoking North Vietnam's powerful supporters, China and the Soviet Union. Although the rules of engagement changed from time to time, for

A low-flying US fighter aircraft casts a shadow near a bomb-shattered road bridge in North Vietnam during the Rolling Thunder bombing campaign.

North Vietnamese women operate a Soviet-supplied anti-aircraft gun. North Vietnam's effective air defences took a heavy toll of US aircraft.

much of the period no attacks were made on Haiphong port, the main entry point for Soviet supplies to North Vietnam.

The bombing cost the United States heavy losses, because the North Vietnamese had Soviet-supplied anti-aircraft guns and missiles, as well as MiG fighter aircraft. The American fliers were forced to observe many limits that restricted them in combat – for example, at first they were not allowed to attack missile sites because they might injure or kill Soviet technicians and thus risk widening the war.

Rolling Thunder is now generally recognized to have been a failure. It inflicted a great deal of damage on North Vietnam's industries, military installations and transport system. It is also reckoned to have killed more than 50,000 civilians. But the bombing had no decisive military effect, while psychologically if anything it stiffened North Vietnamese resistance. It also provided fuel for the anti-war protest movements that arose in the U.S. and internationally in response to the war in Vietnam.

The Rolling Thunder bombing campaign was carried out mostly by US jets flying from South Vietnam and from aircraft carriers, with B-52s also taking part. For fear of bringing China into the war, air strikes were banned close to the Chinese border.

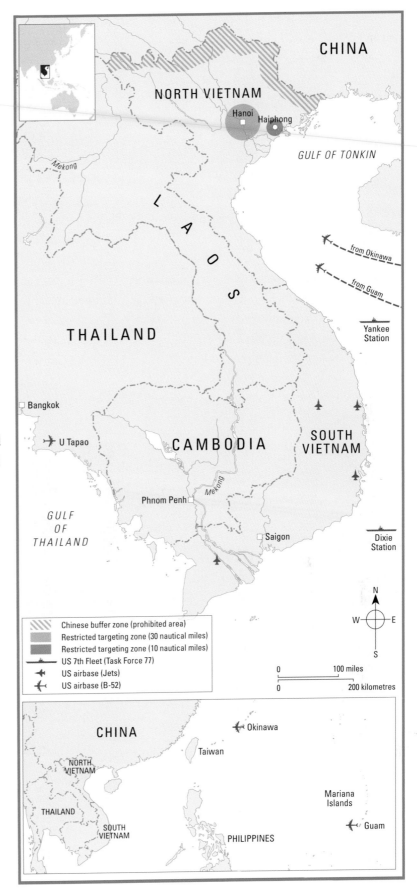

	Chinese buffer zone (prohibited area)
	Restricted targeting zone (30 nautical miles)
	Restricted targeting zone (10 nautical miles)
	US 7th Fleet (Task Force 77)
	US airbase (Jets)
	US airbase (B-52)

CHAPTER 3: SEARCH AND DESTROY – 1965-1967

By 1965 the South Vietnamese government had lost control of most of rural South Vietnam. Around 70 per cent of South Vietnam's villages were in the hands of the communists. The South Vietnamese army – the ARVN – was demoralized and poorly led. It was no match for the communist forces, which now consisted not only of Viet Cong guerrillas but also of soldiers of the North Vietnamese Army (NVA), who had been sent into the South down the Ho Chi Minh Trail. Guerrillas were firmly in control of territory just 30 km from Saigon.

US Marines come ashore from landing craft on a beach in South Vietnam in August 1965. Originally deployed to defend US bases, Marines soon took on an offensive role in Vietnam.

Communist guerrillas dominated large areas of the South Vietnamese countryside in 1965-7. American forces at times penetrated deep inside these hostile areas in the effort to seek out and destroy the enemy.

	Areas under communist control c.1966
	Position of major fighting 1965–7
	US base

0 — 50 miles
0 — 100 kilometres

B-52 bombers, based in Thailand or on the distant islands of Guam or Okinawa, flew many thousands of missions during the war, hitting targets in Vietnam, Cambodia and Laos.

The US government had hoped that if the ARVN troops were given arms and training, they would do the fighting and dying. But now it was clear that only a large-scale commitment of US combat troops could prevent a communist victory. On 8 March 1965, the first combat force of US Marines landed in South Vietnam at Da Nang. By the end of the year there were over 180,000 US military personnel in South Vietnam, supported by an awesome supply operation across the Pacific.

The United States was not the only country to send in troops to defend the South Vietnamese government. Soldiers from Australia, New Zealand, South Korea, Thailand and the Philippines – all members of the South-east Asia Treaty Organization (SEATO) – fought alongside the Americans. But from 1965 until 1969, it was overwhelmingly the United States' war, with these allies and the ARVN itself playing only a relatively marginal part in the fighting. European allies, including Britain, kept out of the Vietnam War.

In theory, the struggle between the forces of the world's greatest military power and lightly armed Viet Cong and NVA infantry appeared one-sided. In reality the US forces, led by General Westmoreland, faced a difficult task. Westmoreland was not allowed to invade North Vietnam, for fear of widening the war, and nor he was not allowed to use nuclear weapons. The US government also refused him permission to send major forces into Laos or Cambodia to block the communist supply routes down South Vietnam's long land border. The Ho Chi Minh Trail was subjected to massive attack by B-52 bombers, but this did not stop the movement of men and supplies. The Viet Cong and NVA were able to replace losses in South Vietnam with fresh arrivals from the North.

With their aircraft, warships and artillery, the Americans deployed a truly amazing quantity and variety of firepower in South Vietnam. In line with traditional US military thinking, Westmoreland believed that the way to win the war was to engage the enemy in combat and use this firepower to destroy the

FULL-SCALE COMMITMENT

Between 1965 and 1968 the US military commitment in Vietnam was at its height, both in terms of numbers of troops and casualties:

	1965	1966	1967	1968
US military personnel	184,300	385,300	485,600	536,100
US deaths in action	1,369	5,008	9,378	14,592

Viet Cong guerrillas move along the waterways of the Mekong Delta, south of Saigon, in 1966. Many villages in the Delta were guerrilla strongholds.

enemy forces. But, unlike in a conventional war, there was no front line where the enemy would stand and fight. Vietnam was a country well suited to guerrilla warfare, whether in the mountainous jungle of the Central Highlands, the waterways of the Mekong Delta, or the densely populated ricefields where guerrillas could hide among the villagers.

Both the Viet Cong and the NVA infantry were elusive, skilled in evading combat until a moment of their own choosing. So Westmoreland developed a strategy of 'search and destroy' – first seek out the enemy, and then call in the firepower.

AIR MOBILITY For mobility, the Americans decided to rely primarily on fleets of helicopters – tanks were regarded as of limited use because, travelling on roads, they were considered too easy to ambush. Helicopters could carry troops rapidly to the point of battle, ferry supplies to firebases deep inside hostile territory, provide a kind of airborne artillery (helicopter gunships), and evacuate the wounded.

The first major test of US forces in South Vietnam came at the battle of the Ia Drang Valley in November

The battle of the Ia Drang Valley began with an NVA attack on a US camp at Plei Me. US troops flew in by helicopter to landing zone X-Ray. After two days' fighting, the NVA withdrew.

1965. This took place in the remote Central Highlands, where the North Vietnamese were building up a substantial body of NVA troops, sent down the Ho Chi Minh Trail. The US command was concerned that the NVA might push down from the Central Highlands to the sea, effectively cutting South Vietnam in half.

The newly formed US 1st Cavalry Division was based in the area, at Ankhe, near Pleiku. With about 400 helicopters, the 1st Cavalry was the US Army's first division created specifically to fight airmobile warfare. A battalion of the 1st Cavalry flew in to relieve a Special Forces base at Plei Me, near the Cambodian border, which had come under NVA attack. A fierce battle was joined between the NVA and the air cavalry. US artillery and aircraft – including B-52 bombers flying in from Guam in the Pacific – subjected the NVA to heavy bombardment. In two days' fighting, the NVA were estimated to have suffered 2,000 casualties, before disappearing back into the jungle.

The US Army rated the Ia Drang Valley a considerable success. It certainly showed that the introduction of US forces was going to prevent any swift communist victory in South Vietnam. But the battle also revealed what a tough fight the Americans had on their hands. At one helicopter Landing Zone (LZ),

a force of 400 US airborne troops, encircled by the NVA, suffered 279 casualties in a day's fighting.

At first the United States fought a primarily defensive campaign, while building up troop strength and logistical support. By the end of 1966, however, with more than 385,000 US soldiers in South Vietnam, Westmoreland was ready to take the offensive with search and destroy operations on a large scale. The aim was to seize control of areas of the country that were currently controlled by the guerrillas, and to inflict heavy losses on the enemy.

One solidly guerrilla-dominated area was between Saigon and the Cambodian border,

POLITICAL WARFARE

Criticizing American policy at this stage of the war, Henry Kissinger, US Secretary of State from 1969 to 1975, wrote:

'We fought a military war; our opponents fought a political one … We lost sight of one of the cardinal [main] maxims of guerrilla war: the guerrilla wins if he does not lose; the conventional army loses if it does not win.'

[Quoted in *America in Vietnam*, Guenter Lewy]

The US Air Cavalry rides into action during an operation in 1967. Before the Vietnam War, helicopters had never been used in mass formation.

including the so-called 'Iron Triangle', a mere 50 km from the South Vietnamese capital. Here the Viet Cong had constructed elaborate systems of tunnels with concealed entrances, making underground fortresses from which their mainforce units could launch attacks on their enemy. The guerrillas could also count on the support of the local villagers, many of whom operated as part-time members of the Viet Cong.

In January 1967 Operation Cedar Falls was launched against the Iron Triangle. It was to be a 'hammer and anvil' operation. US and ARVN troops took up blocking positions on the south-western side of the Triangle, forming the 'anvil'. Helicopter and ground attacks from the north and west would provide the hammer. The Viet Cong were meant to be trapped and crushed between the two.

The operation, lasting nineteen days, went much as planned. The US and ARVN forces occupied the Triangle. Volunteers sent in to explore the networks of

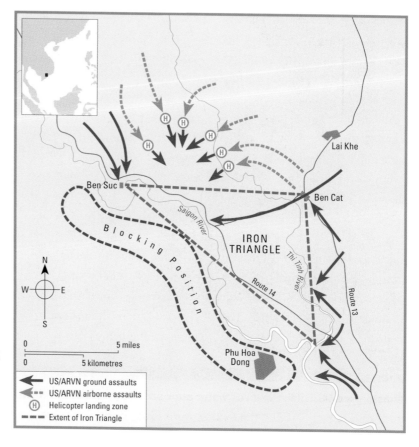

Legend:
← US/ARVN ground assaults
⇠ US/ARVN airborne assaults
Ⓗ Helicopter landing zone
- - - Extent of Iron Triangle

In Operation Cedar Falls in January 1967, US and ARVN troops swept through the Iron Triangle, a Viet Cong stronghold near Saigon. (Below) Men of US 25th Infantry Division leap from a helicopter near Cu Chi during Operation Cedar Falls.

A distressed US soldier is given water after searching one of the tunnels dug by Viet Cong guerrillas in the Iron Triangle near Saigon. The tunnels were subsequently sealed and blown up.

FREE-FIRE ZONE

Villages in South Vietnam were sometimes cleared of their peasant population to create 'free-fire zones'. A US official described this process in 1967:

'The inhabitants are allowed time to pack their belongings and collect their livestock and then are moved to one of the 65 refugee camps in the province. Shortly thereafter the hamlet is destroyed ... friendly forces continue to receive fire from such hamlets and encounter mines, but they are no longer inhibited from returning fire and calling in artillery and air strikes.'

[Quoted in Guerrilla Warfare, Robin Corbett]

bulldozer. Yet the fighting was relatively light, because most of the Viet Cong mainforce managed to disappear into the jungle. Only days after Cedar Falls ended, guerrillas were once more operating in the area.

One of the first American actions in Operation Cedar Falls was the destruction of the village of Ben Suc on the edge of the Triangle. Airborne troops descended on the village, interrogated the population, and arrested suspected Viet Cong members. The villagers were then carried off to a refugee camp and Ben Suc was burned to the ground. Witnessed by journalists, the destruction of the village aroused controversy in the United States, where a vocal anti-war movement was gathering strength.

The fate of Ben Suc was not a one-off event. When the United States took on guerrillas in populated countryside, deploying their massive firepower, the local population inevitably suffered terribly. US forces operated under rules that forbade the unnecessary destruction of civilian lives or property. But often it was unclear who was a civilian and who a guerrilla. If US Army patrols suffered a steady stream of casualties

tunnels – known as 'Tunnel Rats' – unearthed large quantities of supplies and stacks of documents giving details of Viet Cong and NVA military plans. The tunnels were destroyed and areas of forest cleared by

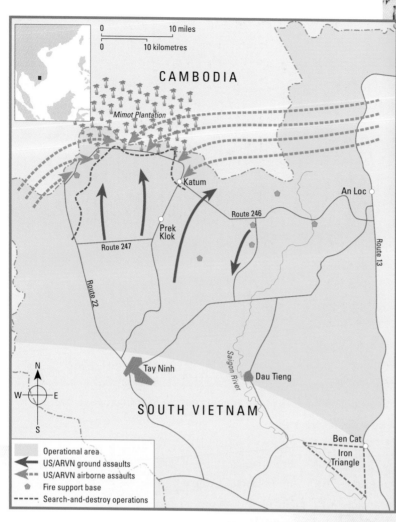

South Vietnamese soldiers discover a dead guerrilla to be added to the 'body count'.

Operation Junction City in spring 1967 was a large-scale search and destroy operation intended to trap the Viet Cong between ground forces and airborne troops landed behind them.

from sniper fire or booby trap bombs in a particular area, the response was often to order the local people to collect their belongings and leave. This created what was called a Free Fire Zone. Anyone who remained behind could be regarded as Viet Cong and treated accordingly. Even when not deliberately driven out, many peasants fled their homes in what had become a battlefield. As a result of the countryside clearance, some 1.5 million South Vietnamese were thought to be living in refugee camps by the end of 1967.

COUNTRYWIDE CONFLICT By that time the number of US military personnel committed to South Vietnam was approaching a half a million. They were fighting from the Mekong Delta in the south – where the US Army and Navy combined in aggressive pushes up rivers in guerrilla territory – to near the border with North Vietnam, where US military outposts came under attack from the NVA. Whenever US forces succeeded in engaging their enemy, they won the fight. But they could never achieve a victory that was in any sense decisive.

US Marines advance through a paddyfield during a search and destroy operation in 1967. Soldiers in rural Vietnam had to be constantly on the watch for snipers or for mines that could kill or maim.

Operation Junction City, in February-April 1967, showed clearly what could and could not be achieved. The operation involved more than 25,000 US and ARVN troops in an attempt to destroy NVA and Viet Cong bases near the Cambodian border. They duly overran the bases and killed around 2,800 enemy – about ten times the casualties they themselves suffered. But they were unable to occupy the area permanently and enemy operations were only briefly disrupted.

Looking for solid evidence of progress in the war, the US government had settled for the 'body count' – regularly updated figures of the number of guerrillas killed in action. Although these figures were undoubtedly exagerrated, they did show the damage that the US forces were able to inflict on the Viet Cong and NVA. But the communists' will to fight on was undaunted. The body count that mattered more to the future of the war was that of US lives lost. By the end of 1967 some 16,000 US servicemen had been killed in Vietnam. The question inevitably was how long Americans would go on accepting these sort of losses. The answer came in 1968.

US troops rush a wounded colleague to a waiting helicopter. Thousands of lives were saved by the speed with which helicopters evacuated casualties.

DISILLUSION WITH WAR

By 1967 US Defense Secretary Robert McNamara had become disillusioned with the war. Before he resigned his post in the autumn of that year, McNamara stated:
'The picture of the world's greatest superpower killing or seriously injuring 1,000 non-combatants a week, while trying to pound a tiny backward nation into submission … is not a pretty one.'
[Quoted in *The Ten Thousand Day War*, Michael Maclear]

CHAPTER 4:
THE DECISIVE YEAR – 1968

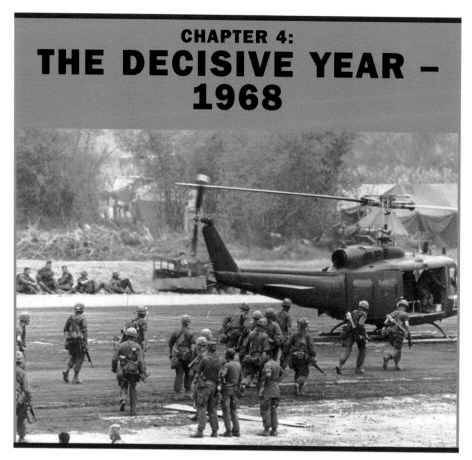

US airborne troops prepare to board a helicopter at a landing zone near Khe Sanh in April 1968.

From January to April 1968 the US Marine base at Khe Sanh was besieged by about 40,000 NVA troops.

By the start of 1968, the North Vietnamese leadership had decided that the time was ripe for a final push to drive the Americans out of South Vietnam. The Viet Cong and NVA guerrillas were ordered to prepare to take over South Vietnam's towns and cities in a coordinated offensive throughout the country. Ho and his colleagues expected that the guerrillas would be welcomed by Vietnamese in the urban areas as liberators and that mass desertions would lead to the collapse of the South Vietnamese army (ARVN).

As a prelude to this offensive, on 21 January 1968 two NVA divisions, numbering around 40,000 troops, laid siege to 5,000 US Marines in a base at Khe Sanh,

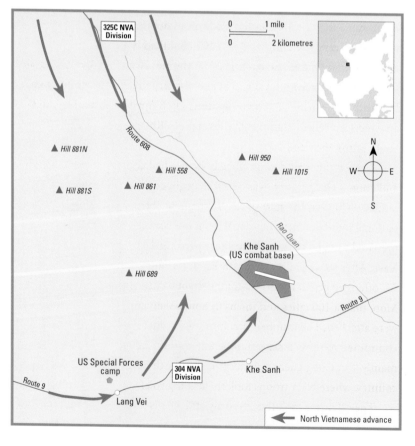

DEVASTATING FIREPOWER

Writing of the part played by airpower in the defence of the base at Khe Sanh, General Westmoreland wrote:

'Without question the amount of firepower put on that piece of real estate exceeded anything that has been seen before in history.'

[Quoted in *Historical Atlas of the Vietnam War,* Harry Summers Jr. and Stanley Karnow]

American soldiers hurry to board a helicopter during the operation to break the siege of Khe Sanh in April 1968.

Two South Vietnamese soldiers take part in the fighting against communist guerrillas in Saigon during the Tet offensive, January 1968.

in the far north of South Vietnam. A repeat of the French defeat at Dien Bien Phu looked possible. The Americans were, however, able to keep the besieged base supplied by air. Round-the-clock air attacks, including heavy bombing by B-52s, battered the NVA troops dug in around the base. The US Marines also took a pounding from NVA rocket and artillery fire, but held firm during 77 days of fighting. On 8 April, an American relief column broke through to Khe Sanh, lifting the siege.

By then the major communist offensive had come and gone. The operation was timed to begin on 30-31 January. This was the start of the Vietnamese Tet national holiday, when the ARVN would be least prepared to fight, with many military personnel on leave. After some preliminary attacks on the 30th, the Tet offensive began in earnest on the night of the 31st. More than a 100 cities and towns in South Vietnam were attacked. The number of communist fighters committed to the offensive numbered around 85,000, mainly Viet Cong guerrillas except in the north of the country, where NVA troops took the leading role.

The offensive took the US Army and ARVN by surprise and initially achieved many of its objectives.

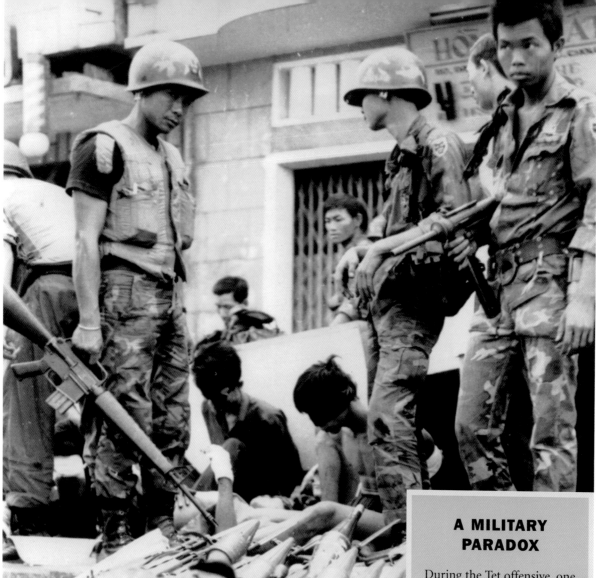

Viet Cong guerrillas, captured by South Vietnamese troops, kneel blindfolded in a Saigon street, February 1968.

In Saigon a platoon of guerrillas broke into the US Embassy compound and larger forces attacked other key military and political installations. Vietnam's former imperial capital, Hue, was occupied by the NVA. But there was no uprising of local people in support of the communists. Counterattacks mounted by the US Army and the ARVN soon recaptured most urban areas – far from collapsing, the ARVN performed far better than expected. Saigon was largely clear of communist fighters within a week. Only Hue was held by the communists for a prolonged period.

Militarily, Tet was a disaster for the Viet Cong and, to a lesser degree, the NVA. The communists probably lost around 30,000 men in the first two weeks of February 1968, compared with around 3,000 of the US Army, ARVN and their allies killed. The fighting of the first half of 1968 as a whole more

A MILITARY PARADOX

During the Tet offensive, one US major involved in retaking the Mekong Delta town of Ben Tre from the Viet Cong allegedly told an interviewer:

We had to destroy the town in order to save it.

[Quoted in *Guerrilla Warfare*, Robin Corbett]

or less destroyed the Viet Cong guerrilla movement, leaving the war to be carried on largely by the NVA.

The political impact of the Tet offensive was, however, disastrous

In the Tet offensive at the end of January 1968, communist forces attacked towns and cities across South Vietnam.

Folk singer Joan Baez, one of the most prominent celebrity anti-war campaigners, takes part in a protest rally in New York.

for the US government. There had been an anti-war movement in the United States since the very start of the Vietnam War. It drew the support of many students and of some prominent individuals, including Civil Rights leader Martin Luther King. They believed America was fighting against a popular liberation movement and doing so in a particularly brutal way. Protests had ranged from large-scale demonstrations to individual refusal to be drafted into the army or the burning of draft cards – the cards sent to people so that they could be called up into the armed forces if required. Among famous people prosecuted for refusing the draft was world boxing champion Muhammad Ali.

But until the Tet offensive the majority of US citizens had continued to support the war effort, if with mounting doubts. Then, after almost three years of large-scale commitment of US forces, the American public saw on their televisions fighting taking place in the streets of South Vietnam's cities and even outside the US embassy. Inevitably, public confidence in the chances of success in the war was severely shaken.

Unknown to the public, the US government had also lost confidence in winning the war. After Tet, with the siege of Khe Sanh and the battle for Hue still

States was no longer seeking victory, but looking for a way out of Vietnam.

The destruction wrought upon South Vietnam during 1968, graphically reported by the media in America and across the world, made an awesome spectacle. In Hue, for example, US Marines and Army soldiers aided by the ARVN fought for more than three weeks to retake the city from the NVA. The house-to-house fighting, plus shelling by US warships, reduced large parts of the city to rubble. The non-combatant dead in Hue included at least 2,800 South Vietnamese government officials, military officers and others rounded up and massacred by the communists.

In the course of 1968 almost 15,000 US

US Marines in action during the street fighting in Hue in spring 1968. About 1,000 Marines were killed or wounded in the battle to retake the city from the NVA.

raging, General Westmoreland requested commitment of another 200,000 US troops to Vietnam. With these extra men – and permission to invade Cambodia and Laos to cut communist supply lines – Westmoreland said that he could win the war. But a report by US Defense Secretary Clark Clifford concluded that: 'All that can be said is that additional troops would enable us to kill more of the enemy …'

ELECTION YEAR 1968 was a presidential election year in the United States. On 31 March 1968 President Johnson announced that he would not stand for re-election. At the same time, the Rolling Thunder bombing raids on North Vietnam were scaled down and the United States sought to open peace negotiations. From that point onwards, the United

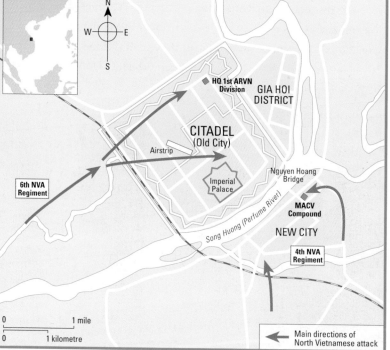

On 31 January 1968 NVA troops attacked the city of Hue. They occupied the old Citadel, apart from the ARVN headquarters, and threatened the MACV Compound, the US headquarters. It took 24 days to retake the Citadel from the NVA.

servicemen were killed in action in Vietnam – nearly 300 a week. The death toll on the communist side almost certainly exceeded 100,000. The number of Vietnamese civilians killed has never been accurately calculated. It is in this context of war at its most brutal that the most notorious atrocity of the conflict took place. On 16 March more than 300 South Vietnamese civilians, including women and children, were massacred in cold blood by American soldiers at the hamlet of My Lai. A number of US officers and NCOs were later prosecuted for their part in the killings, and one, Lieutenant William Calley, was convicted.

The 1968 US presidential election was dominated by the issue of the war. There were violent clashes between anti-war demonstrators and police at the Democrat party convention in Chicago in August. The election was won in November by Republican Richard M. Nixon, who had promised both to 'get tough with the communists' and 'bring our boys back home'.

By then the first steps towards an American withdrawal from Vietnam had already been taken. Refused the extra troops he believed necessary, Westmoreland was replaced as US commander in Vietnam by General Creighton W. Abrams in June 1968. At the end of October, the bombing of North Vietnam was halted. Peace talks were scheduled to begin at the start of 1969. A new phase of the war had begun.

GETTING OUT OF VIETNAM

American author William Broyles Jr., who served as a Marine in Vietnam, wrote:
'There was no single goal in Vietnam; there were 2.8 million goals, one for every American who served there. And in the end the nation's goal became what each soldier's had been all along: to get out of Vietnam.'

[From *Brothers in Arms*, William Broyles]

A man killed in a bombing raid in Hue. Scenes of war such as this, shown on television every evening (for this was the first televised war) helped to stir up anti-war sentiment in the USA.

CHAPTER 5:
VIETNAMIZATION 1969-1971

American soldiers cross a river in the A Shau Valley, rugged country ideal for guerrilla operations.

ATTACKING SPIRIT

General Melvin Zais, commander of the US 101st Airborne Division, vigorously defended the decision to fight for Hamburger Hill:

'That hill was in my area of operations, that was where the enemy was, that's where I attacked him … If I find him on any other hill in the A Shau, I assure you I'll attack him again.'

[Quoted in *America in Vietnam*, Guenter Lewy]

Despite the shocks of Khe Sanh and the Tet offensive, through the second half of 1968 and into 1969 the war went on much as before. US troops continued to carry out major offensive operations to seek out and destroy the enemy. Such operations only came to an end after the battle of the A Shau Valley in May 1969.

The battle began on 10 May when the US 101st Airborne Division flew in by helicopter to take on North Vietnamese troops dug in on the slopes of a hill in the valley, which was close to the border with Laos. A fierce battle was joined as the Airborne Division, soon backed up by other US and ARVN troops, assaulted the NVA positions. The hill was soon nicknamed Hamburger Hill, because of the number of men chewed up on its slopes.

On 20 May the NVA positions were overrun by the US and South Vietnamese – a clear military victory. But the battle for Hamburger Hill caused an outcry in the United States. The US casualties had been 46 dead and some 400 wounded. Earlier in the war, the American public had considered such losses acceptable. In May 1969 they were widely regarded as unacceptably high. US soldiers had also begun to lose their will to fight. From this time onward, morale in many units of the US Army in Vietnam went into sharp decline. Many soldiers had no desire to risk their lives for what was widely regarded as a lost cause.

After Hamburger Hill, the US government, with President Nixon now in charge, ordered General Abrams to avoid any further large-scale battles. In June 1969, Nixon announced the first US troop withdrawals from Vietnam. He declared it a priority that the South Vietnamese Army (ARVN) should take over the prime combat role in the war. This policy was known as 'Vietnamization'.

tasked with turning the ARVN into an efficient fighting force. When Abrams took over from Westmoreland as head of US forces in Vietnam in mid-1968, measures were already afoot for rapidly expanding ARVN troop numbers and improving their equipment.

At the same time, anti-communist South Vietnamese had found a man who could give them some real leadership. General Nguyen Van Thieu had emerged as the most capable of the South Vietnamese generals who vied for power in the mid-1960s. In September 1967 Thieu was confirmed in power by presidential elections which were, by South Vietnamese standards, reasonably free and fair. Although labelled a 'puppet' of the

Richard M. Nixon, US President from 1969 to 1974.

In a sense, there was nothing new about this policy. From the start of its involvement in Vietnam, the official aim of the United States had been to make South Vietnam into a self-sustaining independent country, capable of defending itself. When US troops poured in to the country from 1965 onward, this goal had been for a time largely overlooked as the United States concentrated on direct military confrontation. But back in mid-1967, General Abrams had been

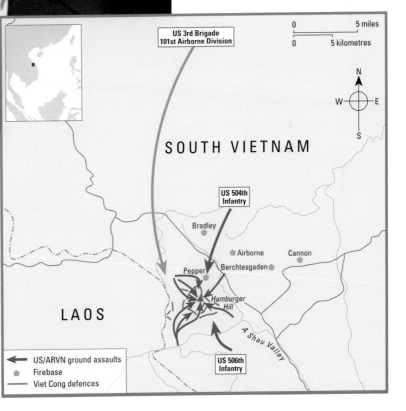

In May 1969 troops of the US 101st Airborne were flown into the A Shau Valley, where they engaged the NVA on Hamburger Hill. After reinforcements were brought in, the hill was captured on 20 May.

Pictures like this – of a US soldier holding a gun to the head of a Vietnamese peasant woman – helped persuade many people that the war was wrong.

United States by the communists and the anti-war movement, Thieu proved a leader of independent spirit who pursued what he regarded as South Vietnam's best interests.

Along with trying to build up the ARVN, the Americans and the South Vietnamese government made progress with the 'pacification' of the South Vietnamese countryside. 'Pacification' meant getting rid of the communist organization in rural South Vietnam and making the country secure under government control. The principal organization behind this effort was CORDS (Civil Operations and Revolutionary Development Support), in which the Central Intelligence Agency (CIA) played a leading role. From the summer of 1968, the pacification campaign had increasing success. In many areas

SCALING BACK

Between 1969 and 1971 the number of US military personnel in Vietnam fell sharply, but combat deaths fell even more steeply:

	1969	**1970**	**1971**
US military personnel	475,200	334,600	156,800
US deaths in action	9,414	4,221	1,380

refugees were resettled on the land and local pro-government militias took responsibility for keeping their villages secure. A land reform programme, distributing land to peasants, helped win their 'hearts and minds'. At the same time, through the ruthless 'Phoenix programme', from 1968 to 1971 thousands of communist activists in South Vietnam were identified and either arrested or killed.

Ironically, by the second half of 1969, when support for the war among the American public was evaporating, the security situation in South Vietnam

By 1971 most densely populated parts of South Vietnam had been brought firmly under government control ('pacified') and fighting with communist forces took place largely in border areas.

US Marines cross the Vu Gia river in pursuit of communist forces in June 1969. By that time, such offensive operations were being phased out as they cost too many American lives.

had vastly improved. Fighting went on mostly in areas close to the border with Cambodia and Laos, away from major centres of population. Heavy losses among South Vietnamese communists, especially in the Tet offensive and the Phoenix programme, had mostly ended the insurgency in South Vietnam. Large areas of the countryside were securely in the government's hands. In North Vietnam, the death of Ho Chi Minh in September 1969 deprived the communists of a national leader of great stature.

Between the second half of 1969 and spring 1972

Young North Vietnamese soldiers who were captured during the incursion into Cambodia in 1970.

the general level of combat in Vietnam was much lower than in the previous four years. American troop levels fell steadily as Nixon fulfilled the promise to 'bring the boys home'. But the troop withdrawals did not mean that the president was prepared to accept a communist victory in Vietnam. While scaling down the troop numbers, Nixon simultaneously widened the war. In March 1969 he secretly authorized the bombing of communist bases in Cambodia by B-52s.

CAMBODIA Since gaining independence from the French, Cambodia had been ruled by Prince Norodom Sihanouk. He had tried to keep his country free of involvement in the war in Vietnam, a policy which had meant turning a blind eye to the presence of Vietnamese communist bases and supply lines in Cambodia. The Nixon administration put pressure on Sihanouk to crack down on the communist presence. Then, in March 1970, Sihanouk was overthrown in a

> **BUYING TIME**
>
> The main aim of the US/South Vietnamese incursion into Cambodia in 1970 was to postpone a major NVA offensive until the ARVN was in a fit condition to defend South Vietnam. President Nixon declared:
> *'We have bought time for the South Vietnamese to strengthen themselves against the enemy.'*
> [Quoted in *Historical Atlas of the Vietnam War*, Harry Summers Jr. and Stanley Karnow]

coup led by the pro-American General Lon Nol.

The bombing and the political instability in Cambodia created a dangerous situation. There were fears that the NVA might attack the Cambodian capital, Phnom Penh. Cambodia also had its own communist guerrilla movement, the Khmer Rouge, which was a growing threat to the government. At the end of April 1970 Nixon authorized a US/South Vietnamese attack across the border from South Vietnam into Cambodia. Aimed at communist bases, the 'incursion' was intended to relieve communist pressure on Phnom Penh and to disrupt NVA preparations for a major attack against South Vietnam. The main targets were two salients known as Parrot's Beak and Fish Hook. Around 25,000 ARVN and US troops, with powerful air support, pushed 30 km inside Cambodia, overrunning communist bases and seizing large quantities of arms and ammunition.

The incursion into Cambodia provoked a wave of anti-war demonstrations across the United States. On 4 May, at Kent State University, Ohio, National Guardsmen shot four student demonstrators dead and wounded 11 others. There was also a hostile reaction in the US Congress, where the Gulf of Tonkin Resolution (see page 14) was repealed and the president was ordered to withdraw US troops from Cambodia by the end of June. In December 1970 Congress banned any further use of US ground troops beyond the borders of South Vietnam. When an incursion into Laos was carried out in January to March 1971 to attack NVA bases and the Ho Chi Minh Trail, only ARVN troops took part, with the support of US aircraft and long-range artillery. The 'Vietnamization' of the war had in effect taken place.

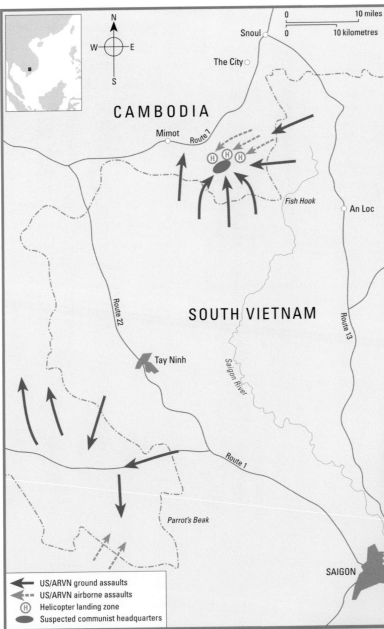

In April-May 1970, US and ARVN forces crossed from South Vietnam into Cambodia to attack communist bases. The incursions targeted the Parrot's Beak and Fish Hook salients.

One of the student anti-war protesters shot dead at Kent State University in May 1970.

CHAPTER 6:
EASTER OFFENSIVE TO CHRISTMAS BOMBING

President Nixon (foreground right) visits Beijing in February 1972. By normalizing America's relations with Communist China, Nixon threatened North Vietnam with potentially losing Chinese support.

Cheerful US Marines embark on the journey home from South Vietnam in March 1971. About 150,000 US soldiers were left in Vietnam by that year's end.

By the start of 1972, peace talks between the warring sides in Vietnam had been under way for three years. The official negotiations, held in Paris, involved representatives of the United States, the South Vietnamese government, the North Vietnamese government and the communist Provisional Revolutionary Government of South Vietnam (PRG). There were also secret meetings between US National Security Adviser Henry Kissinger and the head of the North Vietnamese delegation at the talks, Le Duc Tho. But neither public nor secret negotiations brought any progress towards ending the fighting.

There was, however, diplomatic progress on the wider world stage.

FLIGHT FROM QUANG TRI

A German journalist witnessed the disorganized retreat of South Vietnamese soldiers after the fall of Quang Tri City in May 1972: *'Around noon the first bunch of fleeing soldiers started arriving at the May Chanh bridge … Some were drunk and kept firing wildly into the air. The line of lorries and army vehicles roared on south as if the devil himself were at their heels.'*

[Quoted in *Death in the Ricefields*, Peter Scholl-Latour]

In the NVA's 1972 Easter offensive, the fighting raged around Quang Tri in the north, Kontum in the Central Highlands, and An Loc on the road to Saigon.

President Nixon had undertaken a bold initiative to improve relations between the United States and the two major communist powers, China and the Soviet Union. In February 1972 Nixon became the first US president to visit communist China. North Vietnam was dependent on the major communist powers for arms supplies and diplomatic support. If they grew more friendly with the United States, North Vietnam risked being isolated. This probably influenced the North Vietnamese decision to take a military gamble.

General Vo Nguyen Giap, the North Vietnamese minister of defence, had long been known as a master of guerrilla warfare. But by 1972 he believed the time was ripe to try a new military strategy. With less than 100,000 US military personnel left in South Vietnam

and further withdrawals planned, there was no possibility that US ground forces would be committed again to major fighting. This left the defence of South Vietnam – on the ground at least – in the hands of the ARVN, an army that the North Vietnamese believed they could beat. Giap planned a full-scale invasion of the South by the NVA, using tanks and heavy artillery in support of large troop formations.

The NVA offensive began on Good Friday, 30 March 1972 – for this reason it is often known as the Easter, or Eastertide, offensive. Giap distributed his 130,000 troops on three lines of attack. The offensive opened with a push into Quang Tri Province, immediately south of the DMZ; in early April the NVA struck towards An Loc north of Saigon; and later that

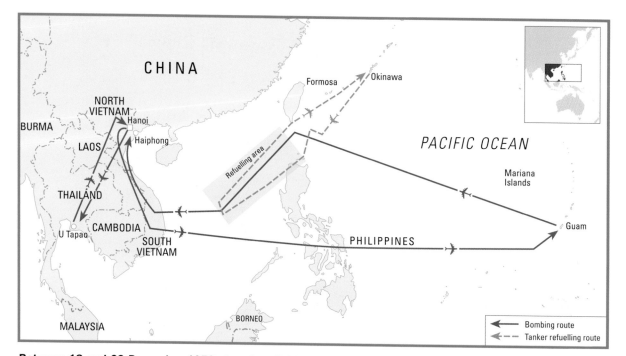

Between 18 and 29 December 1972, American B-52 bombers carried out intensive raids chiefly against targets in the North Vietnamese cities of Hanoi and Haiphong, dropping about 20,000 tonnes of bombs in total. The B-52s based on Guam required in-flight refuelling to achieve the round trip. Other bombers flew from the U Tapao base in Thailand.

month another front was opened in the Central Highlands with a thrust towards Kontum.

The Americans and South Vietnamese had expected a major North Vietnamese attack since the previous year. They had observed the build-up of troops and supplies. But they had been unable to predict the exact timing of the offensive and were largely caught off guard. In places the NVA's use of tanks and long-range artillery caused the South Vietnamese defenders to retreat in near-panic. On each of the three fronts the NVA made gains. By 13 April the North Vietnamese had put An Loc under siege and were advancing towards Saigon, eventually coming within 65 km of the capital. On the northern front, Quang Tri City (see page 39) fell to the NVA on 1 May.

South Vietnamese soldiers inspect the bodies of two of their enemies killed north of Quang Tri in April 1972. Communist losses in the Easter offensive were heavy.

HEAVY BOMBING

On ordering the Linebacker bombing campaign against North Vietnam, President Nixon forthrightly told his advisers: *'The bastards have never been bombed like they're going to be bombed this time.'*
[Quoted by Michael Orr in *War in Peace* magazine, 1984]

By then Kontum was also under threat, raising the prospect of the North Vietnamese advancing down to the coast and cutting South Vietnam in two. The sight of South Vietnamese soldiers and civilian refugees fleeing south from Quang Tri City seemed about to herald the collapse of South Vietnam.

LINEBACKER RAIDS

The United States responded to the offensive by resuming its bombing campaign against the North. The new air campaign was codenamed Linebacker. Having switched from guerrilla to conventional warfare, the NVA now required far more supplies – for example, of fuel and ammunition – to keep the war in the South going. The Linebacker raids struck at the entire North Vietnamese supply chain, including not only roads, bridges and railways, but also fuel depots, ammunition dumps and warehouses in North Vietnam's cities. Most controversially, the entrances to North Vietnamese ports were mined in May to prevent supplies arriving by sea from the Soviet Union. Linebacker was more effective than Rolling Thunder had been, partly because the US air forces now benefited from the introduction of the first laser-guided bombs ('Smart' weapons) and partly because the air operations were less inhibited by politically imposed restrictions on targeting.

People search for survivors in the rubble of a Hanoi hospital, destroyed by a bomb from a B-52 during the Linebacker 2 raids, December 1972. The bomb had been aimed at a nearby barracks.

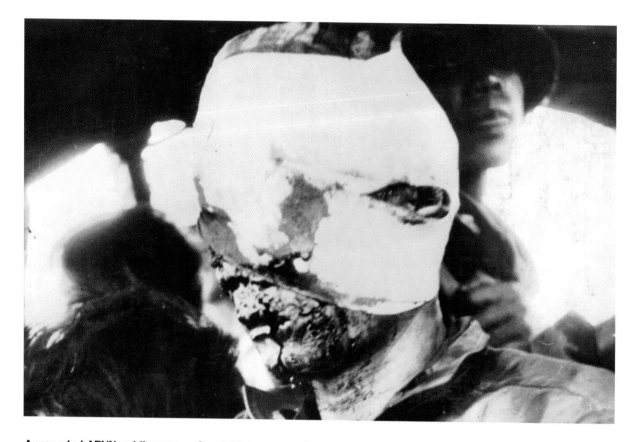

A wounded ARVN soldier: many South Vietnamese who had fought hard felt betrayed by the 1973 peace agreement that allowed the Americans to pull out of the war.

The impact of the Linebacker raids was one factor that contributed to a turn of the tide in the war during May 1972. The performance of the ARVN improved after President Thieu replaced some incompetent generals with better commanders and sent better motivated units to hold key positions. US and South Vietnamese airpower played a decisive role in support of the ground forces, with a variety of strike aircraft, gunships, attack helicopters and bombers hammering the North Vietnamese troops. At An Loc in the second week of May, for example, flights of B-52 bombers struck NVA positions every 55 minutes for almost 30 hours. Along the coast around Quang Tri, firepower from the air was supplemented by the guns of US warships stationed offshore.

The NVA's progress slowed and then halted. An NVA assault on Kontum was driven back at the end of May and by mid-June the siege of An

Loc had been lifted. An ARVN counter-offensive retook Quang Tri City in mid-September. Typically, the soldiers on the communist side fought with remarkable determination under the awesome barrage of bombs, shells and napalm to which they were subjected. But their losses of men and equipment were severe. According to some estimates, around 100,000 NVA troops were killed between March and October 1972 – more than double the losses on the South Vietnamese side. Yet the offensive still left the NVA in possession of significant areas of South Vietnamese territory.

US BOMBING OF NORTH VIETNAM 1972

Linebacker 1 (April-October 1972)

Bombs dropped	156,000 tonnes
US aircraft lost	44

Linebacker 2 (December 1972)

Bombs dropped	20,000 tonnes
US aircraft lost	26 (including 15 B-52s)

Areas controlled by communist forces at time of ceasefire

more stalled, Nixon ordered renewed bombing of North Vietnam on an unprecedented scale. Between 18 and 30 December, a series of raids by B-52s – more than 100 bombers at a time – destroyed almost every target of any military value in Hanoi and Haiphong. Codenamed Linebacker 2, the bombings killed around 1,600 civilians.

In January 1973, peace talks resumed. Agreement was soon reached on terms almost identical to those on the table before the Christmas bombing. A peace deal was formally signed on 27 January. For the United States, the war in Vietnam was over.

The 1973 peace deal allowed the NVA to stay in occupation of areas of South Vietnam that they had seized in the Easter offensive.

Henry Kissinger (facing camera) signs the Paris peace agreement on behalf of the United States, 27 January 1973.

PEACE TREATY

On 22 October 1972 the Linebacker raids were halted and shortly afterwards it was announced that the US and North Vietnam had reached an agreement in principle on a peace deal. The United States would pull out of Vietnam, but North Vietnamese forces would be allowed to stay where they were inside South Vietnam. In return, the North Vietnamese accepted that President Thieu would, for the time being, remain in power in Saigon.

Progress to a signed peace agreement proved far from easy, however. In mid-December, with talks once

CHAPTER 7:
COMMUNISM TRIUMPHANT

US National Security Adviser Henry Kissinger and North Vietnamese negotiator Le Duc Tho were jointly awarded the Nobel Peace Prize for their part in achieving the 1973 peace agreement. Le Duc Tho, however, declined to accept the award, on the grounds that there was no peace. The agreement, in reality, merely opened a new phase of the war. ARVN and NVA forces were fighting small-scale local battles in the week that the agreement was signed.

President Thieu had been very reluctant to sign the peace accord. He felt that an agreement that left 150,000 North Vietnamese troops within his country's borders amounted to a sell-out. Thieu obtained a written assurance from President Nixon that the United States would intervene militarily in support of South Vietnam if the North Vietnamese broke the peace agreement by resuming major offensive action. So, although the last US troops pulled out of Vietnam in March 1973, South Vietnam remained dependent for its survival on American financial aid and on the promise of US military intervention.

South Vietnamese President Nguyen Van Thieu – photographed here with his wife – knew that his country's independence depended on continuing American support, both financial and military.

American prisoners of war are freed by their North Vietnamese captors at Gia Lam airport, Hanoi, in 1973, in accordance with the terms of the Paris peace accords.

TESTING RESOLVE

Gerald Ford, who succeeded Richard Nixon as US President in August 1974, was regarded by the North Vietnamese as a weak leader. A North Vietnamese journalist wrote:

We tested Ford's resolve by attacking Phuoc Long in January 1975. When Ford kept American B-52s in their hangars, our leadership decided on a big offensive against South Vietnam.'

[Quoted in *Historical Atlas of the Vietnam War*, Harry Summers Jr. and Stanley Karnow]

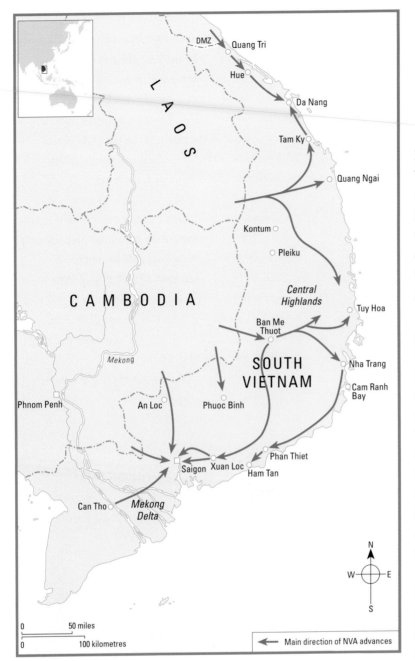

The NVA's victorious offensive in March-April 1975 began with a breakthrough in the Central Highlands, followed by the seizure of the north and a final drive on Saigon.

Nixon was embroiled in the Watergate affair, a political scandal involving illegal entry into the Democratic headquarters during the 1972 presidential election campaign which eventually led to the president's enforced resignation in August 1974.

Meanwhile the balance of power in Vietnam gradually shifted. For most of 1973, the ARVN had the upper hand. US arms rushed in during the period before the peace agreement meant that the South Vietnamese were substantially better equipped than their enemy. The North Vietnamese, for their part, took time to recover both from their losses in the fighting of 1972 and from the damage caused by the US Linebacker bombing campaigns.

But from the end of 1973, the balance began to move decisively in favour of North Vietnam. While the Soviet Union increased its aid to North Vietnam, the US Congress cut back aid to the South. The

It soon became clear that the United States could not be relied upon to fulfil its promises to its South Vietnamese ally. The US Congress, reflecting the mood of the American people, was hostile to any continued military involvement in South-east Asia. In August 1973 a Congressional vote halted the bombing of Cambodia, which had continued after the pull-out from Vietnam. The following November, a War Powers Resolution banned the president from sending US forces into action without the prior approval of Congress. By then,

United States had built up the ARVN into an American-style army, reliant on sophisticated armaments and 'gas-guzzling' vehicles. As money ran short, the South Vietnamese could not afford the spare parts, ammunition and fuel to keep their war machine running.

During 1974 the fighting, although still localized, grew in scale. The ARVN lost some 31,000 troops killed in action in the course of the year. Meanwhile, the North Vietnamese transformed the jungle tracks of

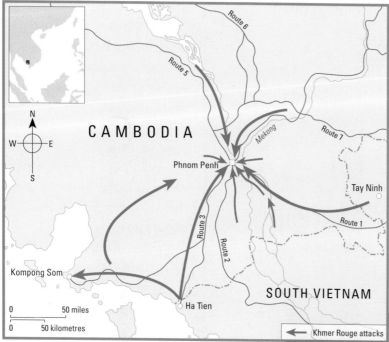

In Cambodia, Khmer Rouge guerrillas advanced from all sides to besiege the capital, Phnom Penh, which fell to the communists on 17 April 1975.

South Vietnamese civilians, desperate to escape the fighting near Xuan Loc in April 1975, struggle to board an ARVN Chinook helicopter as it takes off.

the Ho Chi Minh Trail into a paved road, down which men and supplies poured into their zones of South Vietnam. They even built an oil pipeline into the South to keep their vehicles supplied with fuel.

PUSH FOR VICTORY In December 1974 the North Vietnamese government took the decision to go for military victory. The only thing that might have deterred them would have been renewed American intervention – the Easter offensive had taught them that they could not take over South Vietnam in the face of US airpower. But in January 1975, when the NVA seized a South Vietnamese provincial capital, Phuoc Binh, the United States did nothing. The North Vietnamese leadership concluded that they could safely go ahead with the conquest of South Vietnam.

Commanded by General Van Tien Dung, who had taken over from General Giap, the NVA began the final offensive at the start of March 1975. The main thrust of the attack was through the Central Highlands towards the coast. Poorly led and demoralized, the ARVN forces rapidly disintegrated. By the first week of April, the northern half of South Vietnam was under NVA

NVA soldiers on the balcony of the presidential palace in Saigon look down on North Vietnamese tanks parked in the palace grounds after the communist victory, 30 April 1975.

control. Major cities such as Quang Tri and Hue were abandoned by the ARVN with hardly a fight. Pushing south towards Saigon, the NVA met stiffer resistance. It took them two weeks to overcome ARVN troops at Xuan Loc, north of the capital. But the ultimate outcome of the war was no longer in doubt.

On 21 April President Thieu resigned, denouncing the United States as a country that had 'not honoured its promises'. An evacuation of Americans and selected South Vietnamese from Saigon turned into a race against time as the NVA closed on the city.

The last people to leave were lifted by helicopter from the roof of the US Embassy early on the morning of 30 April. A few hours later, an NVA tank crashed through the gates of the South Vietnamese presidential palace.

In parallel with the collapse of South Vietnam, Cambodia had fallen to communist forces. The Khmer Rouge guerrillas had been within artillery range of the Cambodian capital, Phnom Penh, since early 1974. From the start of 1975, the besieged city was dependent on a US airlift for essential supplies. The defensive perimeter eventually crumbled

'A WAR THAT IS FINISHED ...'

In April 1975, as the NVA closed in on Saigon, President Ford spoke of America's decision not to intervene. He said:

'Today, Americans can regain a sense of pride that existed before Vietnam. But it cannot be achieved by refighting a war that is finished as far as America is concerned.'

[Quoted in *Historical Atlas of the Vietnam War*, Harry Summers Jr. and Stanley Karnow]

after months of sustained pressure, and on 17 April the Khmer Rouge marched into Phnom Penh as victors. By the end of 1975, when the communist Pathet Lao took power in Laos, the whole of former French Indo-China was under communist government.

CHAPTER 6:
AFTERMATH

Spraying large areas of Vietnam with defoliants left a desolate landscape. It may also have caused long-term damage to local people's health.

These are the skulls of Cambodian people killed by the Khmer Rouge. They were found by the Vietnamese after they invaded Cambodia in 1979.

Many well-meaning anti-war campaigners in the United States and elsewhere had hoped that the communists in Indo-China would behave reasonably after victory. These hopes had been encouraged during the war by the North Vietnamese leadership, who had talked of installing a coalition government in South Vietnam, in which communists would share power

with other Vietnamese nationalists. But in fact the two halves of the country were swiftly united as the Socialist Republic of Vietnam under the same communist regime that had ruled North Vietnam. In a significant symbolic gesture, Saigon was renamed Ho Chi Minh City.

More than 200,000 former South Vietnamese officials and army officers were arrested after the communist victory and sent to 're-education camps'. Their treatment was mild, however, compared with that meted out to its former enemies by the Khmer Rouge in Cambodia – now renamed Kampuchea. There, many thousands of supporters of the previous regime were killed. Almost the entire population of Phnom Penh was forcibly relocated to the countryside, where huge numbers died of disease, malnutrition,

ECOLOGICAL DAMAGE

The long-term damage caused to Vietnam by the spraying of defoliants has been a highly controversial issue. According to official US figures:

Total area of Vietnam defoliated 1962-70	5,229,000 acres
Percentage of South Vietnamese forests sprayed 1965-71	46.4 per cent
Percentage of South Vietnamese cultivated land sprayed 1965-71	3.2 per cent

brutal ill-treatment or execution in the 'Killing Fields'.

In former South Vietnam people were also relocated from the cities to the countryside, although with less brutality than witnessed in Kampuchea. Inevitably, life in rural areas was harsh. Anti-personnel mines were scattered around the land and millions of acres had been sprayed with the chemical defoliant Agent Orange, which allegedly caused major long-term health problems (not only for the Vietnamese but also for American Vietnam veterans). In the southern cities, the departure of the Americans brought poverty to thousands who had depended on them for their income. But communist economic policies made matters worse by cracking down on private businesses. In the spring of 1978 thousands of Vietnamese began to flee the country by sea. Many of these 'boat people' were ethnic Chinese, a group who found themselves especially at odds with the communist regime.

If the aftermath of the war was a shock to many Western anti-war campaigners, it also proved a surprise to those, in the United States and elsewhere, who had supported the war as a way of stopping the expansion of the

In winter 1978-9, Vietnam invaded and occupied Kampuchea (Cambodia). China responded by invading Vietnam in February 1979, although the Chinese troops withdrew in March of that year.

Chinese troops direct artillery fire during China's border war with Vietnam in 1979.

'communist bloc'. Instead of communist China and Indo-China forming a united front, perhaps dedicated to expanding communism further across Asia, the communist countries turned to fighting one another.

The Vietnamese had a long history of resistance to Chinese domination. There was also a tradition of hostility between the Khmers – the dominant ethnic group in Kampuchea – and the Vietnamese. Generally submerged during the war against the US and its allies, these tensions resurfaced after the Americans had gone. From 1977, the Khmer Rouge began staging raids into Vietnam in places where the border was disputed. Low-level conflict rumbled on until Christmas 1978, when the Vietnamese mounted a full-scale invasion of Kampuchea. They captured Phnom Penh on 7 January 1979, installing a new government in power. Driven out of the cities, the Khmer Rouge returned to guerrilla warfare, harassing the Vietnamese from bases along the border with Thailand. Vietnamese forces stayed in the country until 1989, when they withdrew to clear the way for a negotiated agreement on the country's future.

WAR WITH CHINA The main backer of the Khmer Rouge regime in Kampuchea had been China. On 17 February 1979, Chinese troops invaded Vietnam. China's intention was not to conquer Vietnam, but to inflict a military defeat to teach the Vietnamese a lesson. In the event, the Chinese army found it hard to make any progress against stiff resistance and withdrew from Vietnam on 6 March.

These events left Vietnam solely reliant on the Soviet Union as a source of foreign aid. The collapse of communism in Eastern Europe in 1989, followed by the break-up of the Soviet Union in 1991, was a huge shock to Vietnam's leaders. Yet the 1990s brought improvement at last in the lives of many of the Vietnamese people. New economic policies, encouraging free enterprise, revitalized Vietnam's cities. In 1995, relations with the United States were at last restored. Vietnam entered the new millennium still under the rule of the communist party, and still extremely poor, especially in rural areas, but with increasing hope for the future.

By then the United States had long emerged from the shadow cast by the Vietnam War. In the 1970s, it seemed that American self-confidence might have been permanently dented by the experience of a conflict from which, for the first time in its history, the United States had not emerged victorious. But with the passage of time, the hostility of the American people to the engagement of US troops in wars abroad weakened. US forces fought in the Gulf War in 1991, and later in Afghanistan and Iraq – although it seemed unlikely that the American people would ever again accept anything like the level of casualties seen in Vietnam.

By the 30th anniversary of the end of America's war in Vietnam, the conflict had become history for a younger generation. To older people, it was part of the living past, still vividly recalled. A major source of income for Vietnam at the start of the twenty-first century was the spending of US tourists, many of them former soldiers revisiting the battlefields where they had fought in their youth.

By 2003 Vietnam was one of only a handful of states across the world still under communist rule.

Communist-ruled states in 2004

NEVER FORGOTTEN

American Vietnam War veteran Lou Carello said: *'The war is never going to be over for me. Any man who fought there is going to go to his grave with that war.'*

[Quoted in *Vietnam: The Ten Thousand Day War*, Michael Maclear]

GENERAL CREIGHTON W. ABRAMS (1914-1974)

Born in Massachusetts in 1914, Abrams had been a US Army officer for thirty years by the time he was appointed deputy commander of MACV in 1967. He took over from General Westmoreland as head of MACV in the summer of 1968 and was in charge during the period of Vietnamization of the war and the withdrawal of US troops. Abrams was appointed US Army chief of staff in 1972, a post he held until his death in 1974.

LIEUTENANT WILLIAM L. CALLEY (1944-)

Aged 23, William Calley dropped out of college in 1966 and enlisted in the US Army. He was sent to Vietnam in November 1967. Calley was a platoon commander at My Lai hamlet in March 1968, when several hundred Vietnamese civilians were massacred. In 1971 Calley was found guilty of the murder of twenty-two civilians, although other officers involved in the incident were cleared. Initially given a life sentence, Calley was only briefly imprisoned. Paroled by President Nixon, he was freed and went on to run his father's jewellery store.

WILLIAM COLBY (1920-1996)

Born in Minnesota in 1920, William Colby devoted most of his life to espionage and undercover activity. He was head of the CIA office in Saigon from 1959 to 1962 and returned to Vietnam in 1968 to head the CORDS pacification programme and the controversial Operation Phoenix. He was subsequently head of the CIA from 1973 to 1975. Colby died, under somewhat mysterious circumstances, in 1996.

EMPEROR BAO DAI (1913-1997)

Born in Hue in 1913, Bao Dai succeeded his father as Emperor of Vietnam – a powerless ceremonial position – in 1925. He abdicated the throne in 1945, but was installed as Vietnamese head of state by the French in 1949. After the peace agreement of 1954, Bao Dai was briefly leader of South Vietnam, but the following year he was replaced by his prime minister, Ngo Dinh Diem. Bao Dai died in exile in France in 1997.

PRESIDENT NGO DINH DIEM (1901-1963)

Born in 1901, Diem belonged to Vietnam's Catholic minority. In 1954 he emerged as the United States' preferred choice of leader for South Vietnam and in October 1955 displaced the former emperor, Bao Dai. Diem's rule was marred by corruption and by favouritism towards Catholics, which brought him into conflict with Vietnam's Buddhist majority. In November 1963 he was overthrown in a military coup approved by the United States. Diem was killed in the course of the coup, along with his brother, Ngo Dinh Nhu.

GENERAL VAN TIEN DUNG (1917-2002)

Born in 1917, Dung joined the Indo-Chinese Communist party in 1937. He played a senior role in the wars against the French and against South Vietnam and the US. In 1974 he was appointed commander-in-chief for the 'Ho Chi Minh' campaign which, the following year, brought about the fall of Saigon. In 1980 he was appointed Vietnam's Minister of Defence. He died in 2002.

PRESIDENT GERALD FORD (1913-)

Born in Nebraska in 1913, Ford was leader of the Republican minority in Congress before becoming US vice-president in 1973 and president in August 1974, on President Richard Nixon's resignation. Hamstrung by the Democrat majority in Congress, in 1975 he was unable to provide extra aid to the South Vietnamese government, let alone authorize a resumption of US military intervention. Ford was defeated in the 1976 presidential election by Jimmy Carter.

GENERAL VO NGUYEN GIAP (1912-)

Giap was born in Quang Binh province in 1912. After joining the Vietnamese Communist Party, he was arrested by the French colonial authorities in 1930 but soon released. In 1939 Giap was ordered by the Party to flee to China to avoid arrest. He joined Ho Chi Minh there. However, his sister-in-law was executed by the French and his wife and child both died in a French prison. From 1942 to 1945 Giap took part in guerrilla warfare against the Japanese in Vietnam, and from 1946 to 1954 he masterminded the Viet Minh campaign against the French, including the victory at Dien Bien Phu. As defence minister in North Vietnam, he directed the guerrilla war against the South Vietnamese government and US forces up to 1972. His decision to resort to conventional warfare in the 1972 Easter offensive, however, led to heavy losses. Although officially still in his post, he was sidelined during the final takeover of the South in 1975.

HO CHI MINH (1892-1969)

Born Nguyen That Thanh in 1892 (although on occasion he also claimed a birth date of 1890), Ho left Vietnam for Europe in 1911 and there, in 1920, became a founding member of the French Communist Party. In 1925 Ho moved to China, where he became the leader of Vietnamese exiles dedicated to freeing their country from French rule. He went back to Vietnam in 1941, founding the Viet Minh guerrilla movement. In 1945 he declared Vietnam independent with himself as president. He led the Viet Minh in the subsequent guerrilla war against France and became president of North Vietnam when the French departed in 1954. He remained the country's leader until his death in 1969.

PRESIDENT LYNDON B. JOHNSON (1908-1973)

Born in Texas in 1908, 'LBJ' was a leading figure in the Democrat Party and became US vice-president under John F. Kennedy in 1961. He assumed the presidency when Kennedy was assassinated in November 1963 and was confirmed in office in presidential elections the following year. Johnson wanted to be a social reformer, transforming the United States into a fairer 'Great Society'. But the Vietnam War diverted money and energy from the reform programme and brought Johnson under increasingly harsh criticism. In March 1968 he announced that he would not stand for re-election. He died in 1973.

PRESIDENT JOHN F. KENNEDY (1917-1963)

Born into a wealthy Catholic family in 1917, Kennedy was decorated for bravery in World War II and subsequently entered politics as a Democrat. In 1960 he narrowly defeated Richard Nixon in presidential elections, becoming his country's youngest ever president. He was responsible for building up the number of US military advisers in South Vietnam from 1961 and approved the overthrow of Diem in November 1963. Kennedy was assassinated three weeks after Diem's downfall. It has been claimed that Kennedy was on the brink of pulling the US out of military involvement in Vietnam when he died, but there is no solid evidence for this.

HENRY KISSINGER (1923-)

Born in Germany in 1923, Henry Kissinger settled in the United States in 1938. He was a leading academic when, in 1969, he was selected by President Nixon to be his adviser on national security. He dominated US foreign policy under Nixon, becoming US Secretary of State in 1973, a post he continued to hold under

President Ford until 1977. Kissinger was awarded the Nobel peace prize, jointly with Le Duc Tho, for his part in negotiating the January 1973 Vietnam peace accord.

ROBERT S. MCNAMARA (1916-)

Born in 1916 in San Francisco, McNamara was president of the Ford Motor Company when, in 1961, he was invited to become secretary of defence in the Kennedy administration. In this post, which he also held under President Lyndon Johnson, McNamara was one of the main architects of the Vietnam War. By 1967, however, he had come to think that the war was a disastrous mistake. He resigned in March 1968 and went on to become president of the World Bank, a position he held until 1981.

GENERAL DUONG VAN MINH (1916-2001)

Known as 'Big Minh', South Vietnamese General Doung Van Minh was one of the leaders of the coup that overthrew President Diem in 1963. After the coup, Minh was South Vietnamese head of government for three months before in his turn being thrown out of power in a coup. In subsequent years Minh was a leading opponent of President Thieu, and an advocate of compromise with the communists. Just before the NVA took Saigon in April 1975, Minh became South Vietnamese president, and it was he who formally surrendered the country to the North Vietnamese.

PRESIDENT RICHARD M. NIXON (1913-1994)

Born in California in 1913, Nixon became US vice-president in 1952, but lost the 1960 presidential election to the Democrat John F. Kennedy. In a remarkable comeback, Nixon was again chosen as Republican presidential

candidate in 1968 and won. Nixon was a tough anti-communist and made forceful use of air power in South-east Asia, but he fulfilled a promise to get US troops out of Vietnam. His diplomatic initiatives also created a new relationship between the USA and communist China and the Soviet Union. After his re-election in 1972, however, he became involved in the Watergate scandal and was forced to resign the presidency to avoid impeachment [being put on trial] in 1974.

GENERAL LON NOL (1913-1985)

Born in 1913, Cambodian General Lon Nol was a leading figure in his country's government from independence in 1955. Under Prince Sihanouk he served as defence minister, army chief of staff and, later, prime minister. In 1970 Lon Nol overthrew Sihanouk in a coup and seized power, but his efforts to crack down on the Khmer Rouge guerrillas were disastrous. He fled Cambodia in 1975, just before the Khmer Rouge victory. Lon Nol died in 1985.

DEAN RUSK (1909-1994)

Born in Georgia in 1909, he held government posts under President Harry Truman after World War II. Rusk was appointed Secretary of State by President Kennedy in 1961 and continued in the same post under President Johnson. He was a crucial decision-maker during the period when the United States was drawn in to full-scale military involvement in Vietnam. Rusk remained secretary of state until President Nixon took office in 1969. He subsequently became a law professor at the University of Georgia.

NORODOM SIHANOUK (1922-)

Born in 1922, Sihanouk was elected king of Cambodia in 1941. When Cambodia gained independence from France in 1955, he abdicated from the throne, but continued to run the country, first as prime minister and then as head of state. In 1970 he was overthrown in a coup and formed a government-in-exile in China. He became an unlikely ally of the communist Khmer Rouge, who made him official head of state again in 1975. After another period in exile from 1979, in 1991 Sihanouk returned to Cambodia once more as head of state – this time opposing the Khmer Rouge – and in 1993 became king again, when the monarchy was restored.

PRESIDENT NGUYEN VAN THIEU (1923-2001)

Born in 1923, Thieu joined the Viet Minh after World War II but soon left because of his opposition to its communist leadership. He then fought for the French in the South Vietnamese Army which, after 1954, became the ARVN. He was one of the leaders of the 1963 coup that overthrew President Diem and took part in the military governments in South Vietnam over the following four years. In 1967 he was elected president as head of a civilian government. Re-elected unopposed in 1971, he only reluctantly agreed to the 1973 peace accords. In 1975 he fled South Vietnam shortly before the fall of Saigon. Thieu died in 2001.

LE DUC THO (1911-1990)

Born in 1911, Le Duc Tho was a founder member of the Indo-Chinese Communist Party in 1930. He played a leading role in the Viet Minh guerrilla campaign against the French and in organizing the guerrilla war in South Vietnam in the 1960s. He acted as a special adviser to the North Vietnamese delegation at the Paris Peace talks, but declined to accept the Nobel peace prize that he was awarded jointly with Henry Kissinger in 1973. He remained a member of Vietnam's ruling politburo until 1986, dying in 1990.

GENERAL WILLIAM C. WESTMORELAND (1914-)

William Westmoreland was born in South Carolina in 1914. By the age of 42 he was a major-general in the US Army. In 1964 he was appointed to command the US forces in Vietnam. Westmoreland followed an aggressive strategy, using large formations of troops to seek out and destroy the enemy. US political leaders, however, became increasingly sceptical of his claims to be winning the war, and the Tet offensive fatally undermined his credibility. In the summer of 1968 Westmoreland was brought back to the United States, where he held the post of army chief of staff until his retirement in 1972.

STATISTICS CONCERNING COMBATANT NATIONS

The figures given below for numbers of armed forces show (where figures are available) firstly the maximum number of personnel from a country that were operating in Vietnam at any one time, and then the total number of people from that country who served in Vietnam from the beginning to the end of the war. Below that are listed the known casualty figures for both troops and civilians (again where available).

AUSTRALIA

Personnel in South Vietnam (max.)	c.8,000
Total Australians who served in South Vietnam (1965-71)	59,520

Casualties

Combat deaths	394
Total deaths	501
Wounded	2,069

REPUBLIC OF KOREA (SOUTH KOREA)

Troops in Vietnam (max.)	47,872
Combat deaths	4,407

NEW ZEALAND

Personnel in South Vietnam (max.)	517
Combat deaths	39

THAILAND

Troops in Vietnam (max.)	c.10,000
Combat deaths	351

UNITED STATES

Personnel (max., 30 April 1969)	543,482
Total US military personnel served in South Vietnam (1964-73)	2,594,000

US Casualties

Combat deaths	47,539
Deaths from other causes	10,797
Total dead	58,336*
Wounded	303,704
Of which severely disabled	75,000

*61 per cent of the Americans killed in Vietnam were 21 years old or younger.

US AIR WAR

Total bombs dropped on South-east Asia	6.7 million tons

(for comparison: total bombs dropped on Germany in World War II 2.7 million tons)

DEMOCRATIC REPUBLIC OF VIETNAM (NORTH VIETNAM)

Armed forces numbers	(1972)
Army	480,000
Air Force	9,000
Navy	3,000
Total combat deaths (including Viet Cong)	440,000
North Vietnamese civilian deaths (est.)	65,000

REPUBLIC OF VIETNAM (SOUTH VIETNAM)

Armed forces numbers (1971)

Regular forces

Army	410,000
Air Force	50,000
Navy	42,000
Marines	14,000
Total regular	516,000

Territorial forces

Regional forces	284,000
Popular forces	248,000
Total territorial	532,000
Grand total	1,048,000

Casualties, South Vietnam

Military deaths (to 1974)	220,357
Military wounded	499,000
Civilian deaths (estimate)	522,000

SIGNIFICANT DATES

1858
France begins conquest of Vietnam.

1930
The Indo-Chinese Communist Party is founded by Ho Chi Minh and others.

1941
The Viet Minh movement is founded to fight for Vietnamese independence.

SEPTEMBER 1945
Ho Chi Minh declares Vietnam independent, with himself as president.

NOVEMBER 1946
French forces drive the Viet Minh out of Hanoi and Haiphong.

1949
Communists under Mao Tse-tung take power in China.

1950-3
Armed by China, the Viet Minh fight against the French.

MARCH-MAY 1954
The French are defeated by the Viet Minh at Dien Bien Phu.

JULY 1954
Geneva peace accords end the First Indo-China War. Ho Chi Minh and his colleagues take power in North Vietnam.

OCTOBER 1955
In South Vietnam, Ngo Dinh Diem defeats former emperor Bao Dai in a referendum and declares himself president of the Republic of Vietnam.

1959
Guerrilla war begins in the South, backed by North Vietnam.

1960
Communists found the National Liberation Front (NLF) to coordinate the guerrilla struggle.

1961
President Kennedy sends first US Army helicopter pilots to South Vietnam.

1962
US Special Forces – the Green Berets – are deployed in South Vietnam.

MAY 1963
Serious clashes between Vietnamese Buddhists and the Diem regime.

2 NOVEMBER 1963
Diem is killed in the course of a military coup.

22 NOVEMBER 1963
President Kennedy is assassinated in Dallas, Texas; Lyndon B. Johnson becomes President of the United States.

MAY 1964
General Westmoreland is appointed commander of US forces in Vietnam.

AUGUST 1964
Reports of attacks by the North Vietnamese on US warships in the Gulf of Tonkin lead to a resolution in US Congress authorizing military action in Vietnam.

FEBRUARY 1965
US launches air strikes on North Vietnam in retaliation for guerrilla attacks on US bases in South Vietnam.

MARCH 1965
First US Marines land in South Vietnam, officially to defend US bases; Rolling Thunder bombing campaign against the North begins.

NOVEMBER 1965
Battle of Ia Drang Valley, first major encounter between the US Army and the NVA.

1966
US troop levels in Vietnam rise to 385,000; US death toll for the year tops 5,000.

JANUARY 1967
Operation Cedar Falls attacks the guerrilla-dominated Iron Triangle.

FEBRUARY-MAY 1967
Operation Junction City targets communist bases near the Cambodian border.

MAY 1967
Civil Operations and Rural Development Support (CORDS) is established, an organization dedicated to the 'pacification' of rural South Vietnam.

SEPTEMBER 1967
Nguyen Van Thieu wins presidential election in South Vietnam.

OCTOBER 1967
Thousands of US anti-war protesters gather around the Pentagon in Washington DC to condemn the war.

JANUARY-APRIL 1968
Siege of the US Marine base at Khe Sanh.

JANUARY-FEBRUARY 1968
Viet Cong and NVA attack South Vietnamese towns and cities in the Tet offensive.

MARCH 1968
Robert McNamara resigns as US Defense Secretary; President Johnson announces that he will not stand for re-election as president.

JULY 1968
General Abrams replaces General Westmoreland as commander of US forces in Vietnam; the Phoenix programme is instigated, targeting communist activists in South Vietnam.

AUGUST 1968
Anti-war protesters battle with US police in Chicago during the Democratic convention.

OCTOBER 1968
Bombing of North Vietnam is halted.

NOVEMBER 1968
Richard Nixon wins US presidential election.

JANUARY 1969
Peace talks begin in Paris.

MARCH 1969
Nixon authorizes the secret bombing of Cambodia.

APRIL 1969
US troop levels in Vietnam peak at 543,482.

MAY 1969
Battle of Hamburger Hill in the A Shau Valley.

JUNE 1969
Nixon announces the first US troop withdrawals and that priority is to be given to 'Vietnamization'.

SEPTEMBER 1969
The president of North Vietnam Ho Chi Minh dies.

MARCH 1970
In Cambodia, General Lon Nol takes power in a coup that deposes Norodom Sihanouk.

APRIL-JUNE 1970
US and ARVN forces carry out an 'incursion' into Cambodia.

4 MAY 1970
Four young anti-war demonstrators are shot dead by the US National Guard at Kent State University, Ohio.

JUNE 1970
US Congress repeals the Gulf of Tonkin Resolution.

JANUARY-APRIL 1971
ARVN forces carry out incursion into Laos.

MARCH 1971
Lt. William Calley is found guilty of killings of Vietnamese civilians at My Lai in March 1968.

AUGUST 1971
Australia and New Zealand announce withdrawal of troops from Vietnam.

FEBRUARY 1972
President Nixon visits China and holds talks with Chairman Mao.

30 MARCH 1972
North Vietnam opens its Easter Offensive against the South.

APRIL-OCTOBER 1972
US Linebacker 1 air bombing campaign against North Vietnam.

APRIL-JULY 1972
NVA siege of An Loc resisted by ARVN with support of US airpower.

1 MAY 1972
Quang Tri City falls to the NVA.

16 SEPTEMBER 1972
Quang Tri City recaptured by ARVN.

OCTOBER 1972
Breakthrough announced in Paris peace talks.

18-30 DECEMBER 1972
B-52 bombers batter North Vietnamese cities in Operation Linebacker 2.

27 JANUARY 1973
Peace agreement signed in Paris.

29 MARCH 1973
Last US troops leave Vietnam.

AUGUST 1973
US Congress forces a halt to the bombing of Cambodia.

AUGUST 1974
President Nixon resigns because of the Watergate scandal; Gerald Ford becomes president.

SEPTEMBER 1974
President Ford announces a partial amnesty for Vietnam War deserters and draft evaders.

JANUARY 1975
The NVA seizes a South Vietnamese provincial capital, Phuoc Binh. The North Vietnamese leadership approves a plan for the final defeat of South Vietnam.

MARCH 1975
The ARVN crumbles in the face of an NVA offensive; the northern half of South Vietnam is abandoned to the NVA.

17 APRIL 1975
The Cambodian capital Phnom Penh falls to the Khmer Rouge.

21 APRIL 1975
President Thieu resigns as NVA forces approach Saigon.

30 APRIL 1975
The NVA enters Saigon as the last US personnel flee; South Vietnam surrenders.

DECEMBER 1975
Laos becomes a communist People's Democratic Republic.

1976
The Socialist Republic of Vietnam is founded; Saigon becomes Ho Chi Minh City.

JANUARY 1977
President Jimmy Carter pardons most Vietnam War draft evaders.

DECEMBER 1978
Vietnam invades Kampuchea (Cambodia), ousting the Khmer Rouge regime the following month.

FEBRUARY-MARCH 1979
Border war between China and Vietnam.

1989
Vietnamese forces withdraw from Cambodia.

1995
Relations between Vietnam and the United States are normalized.

GLOSSARY

17th parallel Line of latitude 17 degrees north of the equator, chosen as dividing line between North and South Vietnam.

air cavalry US troop formations using fleets of helicopters to advance to the battlefield.

airlift Delivery of supplies or troops by air.

airmobile Term used for US troops normally moving around by helicopter.

ARVN Army of the Republic of Vietnam – the South Vietnamese army.

atrocity Massacre or other act of extreme brutality, especially against civilians in wartime.

besieged Encircled by an enemy.

CIA Central Intelligence Agency, the US organization dedicated to carry out espionage and covert operations abroad.

CIDGs Civilian Irregular Defense Groups – guerrilla forces organized by US Special Forces in remote areas of South Vietnam.

coalition Government in which more than one political party takes part and has a share in power.

colony A country ruled by another country as part of its empire.

communists People who believe in a state that is run by a single party that means to build a new society based on economic equality and the state ownership of property.

concentration camp A guarded enclosure in which people are imprisoned.

conventional warfare As opposed to guerrilla warfare, the use of regular armed forces fighting in the open with heavy arms and equipment.

CORDS Civil Operations and Revolutionary Development Support – organization set up by the Americans in South Vietnam to encourage loyalty to the South Vietnamese government among the rural population.

counter-insurgency Operations to suppress a guerrilla movement.

coup The overthrow of one government and the setting up of another, usually by army officers.

covert Carried out in secret.

defoliants Chemicals that kill plants by destroying their leaves.

democratic Term used for a government that is freely elected by a country's citizens.

DMZ Demilitarized Zone – area on each side of the border between North and South Vietnam where military forces were not supposed to operate.

domino theory The idea that if one country in Asia became a communist state, other Asian countries would soon follow, like a line of dominoes falling down when one of them is pushed over.

draft Compulsory military service.

escalate To raise in level or scale.

ethnic A term used to describe people belonging to a particular group by birth, as in 'ethnic Chinese'.

firebase A base where heavy artillery was stationed to provide supporting fire for infantry patrolling the surrounding countryside.

guerrillas Soldiers who are not part of a regular army and who use surprise attacks and concealment in fighting a more heavily armed enemy.

gunships Fixed-wing aircraft or helicopters

armed with a powerful array of guns and missiles, used to attack troops on the ground.

impeachment In the United States, putting the president on trial for crimes.

imperialist A term used to describe one country when it dominates or rules another.

insurgency Revolt or rebellion against government authority.

intelligence In a military context, secret information about enemy movements or plans.

Khmer Rouge Communist guerrilla organization in Cambodia that ruled the country (as Kampuchea) 1975-9.

logistical support The supplies of ammunition, food, fuel etc. needed to keep an army in operation on the battlefield.

MACV Military Assistance Command, Vietnam – the US headquarters in South Vietnam.

militia A body of civilians who are armed to defend their locality.

napalm Inflammable liquid, dropped from aircraft as firebombs (some 400,000 tons of napalm were dropped in the Vietnam War).

nationalist In Vietnam, a term for those who wanted Vietnam to be an independent, unified nation.

NLF National Liberation Front – the South Vietnamese guerrilla movement.

NVA North Vietnamese Army.

pacification Term used to describe the establishment of secure government control over areas where guerrillas have been active.

personnel, military All people working for the various armed forces of a country.

politburo Short for 'political bureau', the ruling committee that in communist countries, such as North Vietnam, often held effective power.

power vacuum The situation in which, temporarily, no government is in control of a country.

regime Government or system of government.

resolution A formal proposal agreed by a vote.

salient A place where a border or a front line sticks out or bulges into foreign or enemy-held territory.

self-sustaining Capable of keeping going without needing outside support.

smart weapons Bombs or missiles with sophisticated guidance systems that give a high level of accuracy against a target.

sorties Raids by those under siege against the besieging enemy.

subversion Activities designed to undermine a government's authority.

VC Viet Cong – term used for communist guerrillas operating in South Vietnam.

FURTHER INFORMATION

RECOMMENDED BOOKS

For young readers, the most accessible fuller books on the war are:

Hall, Mitchel K. *The Vietnam War* (Longman, 1999)

Sanders, Vivienne *The USA and Vietnam 1945-75* (Hodder Arnold, 2002)

Larger-scale historical, biographical and journalistic books about the war include the following titles. While they may contain more information than younger readers can digest in their entirety, using the contents page or index of each book is a good way of finding out more about a particular battle or aspect of the war.

Corbett, Robin *Guerrilla Warfare* (London, 1986)

Currey, Cecil B. *Victory at Any Cost: the Genius of Viet Nam's General Vo Nguyen Giap* (London, 2000)

Fall, Bernard *Street Without Joy* (London, 1961) (a classic book on the First Indo-China War)

Fenn, Charles *Ho Chi Minh* (London, 1973)

Karnow, Stanley *Vietnam: A History* (New York, 1983)

Lewy, Guenter *America in Vietnam* (Oxford, 1978)

Maclear, Michael *Vietnam: The Ten Thousand Day War* (London, 1981)

Mann, Robert *A Grand Delusion: America's Descent into Vietnam* (New York, 2001)

Scholl-Latour, Peter *Death in the Rice Fields* (New York, 1979)

Sheehan, Neil *A Bright Shining Lie* (New York, 1988)

Summers, Harry G. Jr. *Historical Atlas of the Vietnam War* (Boston, 1995)

There are many published first-hand accounts – or collections of first-hand accounts – of the Vietnam experience. Among the best are:

Barker, Mark *Nam* (London, 1987)

Broyles, William Jr. *Brothers in Arms: A Journey from War to Peace* (New York, 1986)

Caputo, Philip *A Rumor of War* (Pimlico, 1999)

Donovan, David *Once a Warrior King: Memories of an Officer in Vietnam* (Corgi, 1981)

Mason, Robert *Chickenhawk* (Corgi, 1984)

Moore, Harold G. and Galloway, Joseph L. *We Were Soldiers Once... and Young* (New York, 1992)

O'Brien, Tim *If I Die in a Combat Zone* (Flamingo, 1989)

For a flavour of the anti-war movement, it is best to turn to books written at the time. Among the most readable still available are:

McCarthy, Mary *Vietnam* (Penguin, 1968)

Mailer, Norman *Miami Beach and the Siege of Chicago* (Penguin, 1971)

SOURCES OF QUOTATIONS

America in Vietnam, Guenter Lewy, Oxford, 1978.

Brothers in Arms: A Journey from War to Peace, William Broyles Jr., New York, 1986.

Death in the Rice Fields, Peter Scholl-Latour, New York, 1979.

Guerrilla Warfare, Robin Corbett, London, 1986.

Historical Atlas of the Vietnam War, Harry G. Summers Jr., Boston, 1995.

Vietnam: The Ten Thousand Day War, Michael Maclear, London, 1981.

War in Peace magazine, London, 1984

RECOMMENDED FILMS AND TV

Many films have been set in the Vietnam War. Most contain strong language and, almost inevitably, extreme violence. So the following information is given on the understanding that younger readers would need to obtain parental permission before viewing these films. The movies are made from an American viewpoint and none can claim to present a balanced view of the Vietnam experience, but they are worth watching to gain an impression of what the war was like. All are available on video.

Apocalypse Now (1979)
The Deer Hunter (1978)
Good Morning, Vietnam (1987)
Platoon (1986)

Vietnam: A Television History, produced by WGBH, Boston, is available on video.

RECOMMENDED WEBSITES

www.spartacus.schoolnet.co.uk/vietnam.html
Covers personalities, events and issues of the war, as well as providing links.

www.pbs.org/wgbh/amex/vietnam
Part of the WGBH American Experience series, 'Vietnam Online' includes an interactive timeline among its many features.

www.lcweb.loc.gov/folklife/vets
An official oral history website, the Veterans History Project, includes fascinating first-hand accounts of the war. Intelligently organized.

http://web.uccs.edu/~history/index/vietnam.html
A guide to resources and research sources available on the Web.

www.WomenInVietnam.com
Tries to rectify the general neglect of women's role in the Vietnam War.

Note to parents and teachers
Every effort has been made by the publishers to ensure that these websites are suitable for children; that they are of the highest educational value; and that they contain no inappropriate or offensive material.

However, because of the nature of the Internet, it is impossible to guarantee that the contents of these sites will not be altered. We strongly advise that Internet access is supervised by a responsible adult.

PLACES TO VISIT

The National Vietnam Veterans Memorial in Washington D.C.
Popularly known as 'The Wall', this black granite structure is engraved with the names of more than 58,000 members of the US armed forces killed or missing in action in the Vietnam War.

The Vietnam Veteran's Memorial and The Vietnam Era Educational Center
Exit 116, Garden State Parkway
Holmdel, New Jersey.
For group tours and additional information, see their website: http://www.njvvmf.org/

National Vietnam Veterans Art Museum
1801 South Indiana Avenue
Chicago
Illinois 60616.
Tel: 312-326-0270
Fax: 31-326-9767
Website: http://www.nvvam.org/

Gallery Vietnam
55 N. Moore Street
New York, NY 10013
Tel: 212-431-8889
Fax 212-202-4737
http//www.galleryvietnam.com

INDEX

Numbers in **bold** refer to captions to pictures or, where indicated, to maps.

17th parallel 9, **9**

A Shau Valley 32, **32, 33**
Abrams, General Creighton W. 31, 32, 33, 52
Afghanistan 50
Agent Orange 49
air cavalry 21
air mobility 20
air strikes **15**, 16, **17**
    Rolling Thunder **17 map**
airborne troops 24
aircraft carriers **17**
Ali, Muhammad 29
American withdrawal from
    Vietnam 31
Ankhe 20
An Loc 39, **39**, 40, 42
Annam **7**
anti-personnel mines 49
anti-aircraft guns **16**, 17
anti-war demonstrations 17, 31, 37, **37**
anti-war movement 29, **31**
artillery 8
ARVN (Army of the Republic of
    Vietnam) 10, 12, **12**, 13, 18, 19, 22, 25, 26, 27, 28, 32, 33, 34, 37, 39, 44, 45, 47
ARVN soldier, wounded **42**
Australia 19

B-52 bombers **17**, 19, **19**, 21, 27, 36, **40, 41**, 42, 43, **44**
Baez, Joan **29**
Bao Dai, Emperor *see* Dai,
    Emperor Bao
Bejing 38
Ben Suc 23
Ben Tre **28**
Bien Hoa airbase 13, **17**
Bigeard, Major Marcel **6**

boat people 49
body count **24**, 25
bomb **17, 41**
    damage in North Vietnam 16
bombing 17
bombing raids **31, 40**
booby-trap bombs 13, 25
Broyles, William Jr. **31**
Buddhist monk, public suicide of
    14, **14**
Buddhists 10, 14, **14**,
bufferzone on Chinese border **17**
    map

Calley, Lieutenant William 31, 52
Cambodia 4, 8, 11, **11**, 19, **19**, 30, 35, 36, **36**, 37, 45, **46**, 47
    bombing of communist bases in
    36
Cambodian people, skulls of **48**
Can Lao 11
Carello, Lou **51**
ceasefire 1972, areas controlled by
    communists **43 map**
Cedar Falls, Operation 22, **22 map**, **22**, 23
Central Highlands 20, **45**
chemical defoliants 13, **13**
China 6, 7, 16, **17, 49**
Chinook helicopter **46**
CIA (Central Intelligence Agency)
    34
Civilian Irregular Defense Groups
    (CIDGs) 13
Clifford, US Defense Secretary
    Clark 30
Cochin China **7**
Colby, William 52
communism 7, 10
communist 4, 5, 15, 18, 48, **51**
    activity, areas of 1969-71 **35**
    map
Communist China **38**
communist states in 1950s **5 map**
Constellation, USS 16
CORDS (Civil Operations and

Revolutionary Development
    Support) 34
counter-insurgency 13
covert operations 15
Cu Chi **22**

Dai, Emperor Bao 7, 9, 52
Da Nang 19
dead body **31**
defoliant spraying 13, 14, 48, **48**
Dhan, Tran Ngoc **4**
Diem, President Ngo Dinh **10**, 11, 14, **14**, 52
Diem, Nhu 14
Dien Bien Phu 7, **7**, 8, **8**, **9**, 27
    French defences overrun at 8
domino theory **11**
Duong Van Minh, President *see*
    Minh, President Duong Van
Dung, General Van Tien 46, 52

Easter (or Eastertide) offensive
    1972 39, **39 map**, **39**, 40, **43**, 46
Eisenhower, President Dwight D. 8, **9**

firepower 19
Fish Hook 37, **37**, **37 map**
Ford, President Gerald **44**, **47**, 52
France 4, 6, 8
Free-fire zone **23**, 25
French Indo-China 4, **4**, 5, **5**
    in 1950s **5 map**
French paratroopers **8**

Geneva 8
Geneva Accords 8, 9
Gia Lam airport **44**
Giap, General Vo Nguyen 5, 39, 46, 52
Green Berets 13
Guam **19**, 20, **40**
guerrilla army 12
guerrillas 13, **13**, 18, 20, 21, 22, 23, 25, 26
    areas held by c.1960 **11 map**

communist-led **10, 18,** 27
dead **24**
operations **32**
Viet Cong **23, 28**
guerrilla warfare 6, 11, 20
Gulf of Tonkin *see* Tonkin, Gulf of
Gulf War 50

Haiphong 6, 17, **40,** 43
Hamburger Hill 32, **33**
battle for **33 map**
Hanoi 5, 6, **40,** 43, **44**
bombed hospital in **41**
helicopter pilots 13
helicopters 20, **21, 26,** 27
evacuating casualties **25**
Ho Chi Minh 4, **4, 8,** 9, 26, 35, 53
Ho Chi Minh City 48
Ho Chi Minh trail 11, 18, 19, 20,
37, 46
Hue 28, **31,** 47
battle for 29, **30 map**
MACV compound in **30**

Ia Drang Valley, battle of 20, **20,** 21
incursion into Cambodia in 1970
36, 37, **37 map**
incursion into Laos 37
Indo-China 10
Iraq 50
Iron Triangle 22, **22 map, 22,** 23

Japan 4, 5
Japanese troops **4**
occupy Vietnam, 1941 4, **4**
Johnson, President Lyndon B. 14,
15, **15,** 16, 30, 53
Junction City, Operation **24 map,
24,** 25

Kampuchea 48, 49, **49,** 50
Vietnamese invasion of **49 map,**
50
Kent State University, Ohio 37, **37**
Kennedy, President John F. **11,** 13,
14, 53
Khe Sanh 26, **26,** 27, **27,** 29, 32
siege of **26 map,** 27
'Killing Fields' 49
King, Martin Luther 29

Kissinger, US National Security
Adviser Henry **21,** 38, **43,** 44, 53
Khmer Rouge 36, 48, **48,** 50
guerrillas **46,** 47
Khmers 50
Kontum **39, 40,** 41, 42

landing craft **18**
Laos 4, 8, 11, **11,** 15, 19, **19,** 30, 35,
47
Le Duc Tho *see* Tho, Le Duc
League for the Independence of
Vietnam 4
Linebacker bombing raids 1972 **40
map,** 41, **41,** 42, 43, 45
Linebacker 1 **42**
Linebacker 2 raids **41, 42**
long-range artillery 40
Lon Nol *see* Nol, General Lon

MACV *see* Military Assistance
Command Vietnam
Maddox, USS 15, **15, 15 map,** 16
Mao Tse-tung *see* Tse-Tung, Mao
Marines, US see US Marines
McNamara, Secretary of Defense
Robert 15, **25,** 53
Mekong Delta 11, 20, **20,** 25
MiG fighter aircraft 17
Minh, General Duong Van 14, 53
Minh, Ho Chi *see* Ho Chi Minh
mission, chemical defoliant **13**
military advisers 13, 15
Military Assistance Advisory
Group 10
Military Assistance Command
Vietnam – MACV 10, 15, **30**
Military personnel in Vietnam 55
(*see also* US military personnel)
Montagnard communities **12 map**
Montagnard tribespeople 13
morale 32
My Lai massacre 31

napalm 42
National Liberation Front (NLF)
11
Navarre, General Henri **9**
New Zealand 19
Ngo Dinh Diem *see* Diem,

President Ngo Dinh
Nguyen Van Thieu *see* Thieu,
General Nguyen Van
Nixon, President Richard M. 31,
32, **33,** 36, **38,** 39, **41,** 43, 44, 53-4
NLF *see* National Liberation Front
Nobel Peace Prize 44
Nol, General Lon 36, 54
Norodom Sihanouk *see* Sihanouk,
Prince Norodom
North Korea 7, 15
North Vietnam 9, **9,** 10, 11, 15, 16,
39
bomb damage in **16**
establishment of **9 map**
US bombing of 16
North Vietnamese **16**
North Vietnamese Army (NVA) 18,
19, 20, 21, 23, 25, 26, **26,** 27, 28,
29, **30,** 32, 36, 37, 40, 41, **43,** 44,
45, 46, 47
1975 offensive against South
Vietnam **45 map,** 46
bases 25
troops killed March to October
1972 42
North Vietnamese ports, mining of
41
North Vietnamese soldiers, **47**
captured **36**
supply chain of 41
NVA *see* North Vietnamese Army

occupation of Vietnam by Japan **4**
Okinawa 19

'pacification' 34, 35
programme in South Vietnam **35
map**
Paris 38
Parrot's Beak 37, **37, 37 map**
Pathet Lao 47
peace accord, Paris **44**
peace agreement **42**
peace deal, 1973 **43**
negotiations 30, 38
peace treaty, signed in Paris 43, **43**
Philippines 19
Phoenix programme 34, 35
Phnom Penh 36, **46,** 47, 48, 50

Phuoc Binh 46
Phuoc Long **44**
Plei Me 20, **20**,
Pleiku 20
policies, new economic 50
protest rally, anti-war **29**
Provisional Revolutionary
    Government of South Vietnam
    (PRG) 38

Quang Tri City 40, **40**, 41, 42, 47
Quang Tri Province 39, **39**,

Red River Delta 6
re-education camps 48
refugee camps 25
refugees from fighting **46**
Rolling Thunder, Operation 16, **16**,
    17, **17**, 30, 41
    statistics concerning **16**
    target zones **17 map**
Rusk, Dean 54

Saigon 5, 10, 13, 15, 18, **20, 22, 23**,
    27, 28, 40, 43, 47
    evacuation of 47
    fall of **45 map, 45**
    presidential palace occupied in
    47
Search and destroy operations 20,
    21, **25**
SEATO *see* South East Asia Treaty
    Organization
Servicemen killed in action 30
Sihanouk, Prince Norodom 36, 54
'Smart' weapons 41
South East Asia Treaty
    Organization (SEATO) 19
South Korea 7, 19
South Vietnam 9, **9**, 10, 11, 15, **17**,
    18, 21, 33, 46
    areas of under communist
    control in 1966 **18 map**
    establishment of **9 map**
    military personnel in 19
    troops in **12**
    Vietnamese soldiers **10**
    US bases in 1966 **18 map**
Soviet Union 16, 45, 50
    break-up of 50

Special Forces, US detachments in
    Vietnam **12 map**
Strategic Hamlets programme 13
supply routes **11**
    North to South Vietnam **11 map**

terrorist attacks 11
Tet offensive, 1968 27, **27**, 28, 29,
    29 map, 29, 32, 35
Thailand 19, **19**
Thieu, General Nguyen Van 33, 34,
    42, 43, 44, **44**, 47, 54
Tho, Le Duc 38, 44, 54
Ticonderoga, USS 15, 16
Tonkin **7**
Tonkin, Gulf of 15
    incident **15, 15 map**
    naval actions in **15 map**
    Resolution 14, 16, 37
troop withdrawal 36
Tse-tung, Mao 6
Tran Ngoc Danh *see* Danh, Tran
    Ngoc
tunnel rats 23
tunnels 22, **23**

United States 5, 6, 8, 10, 17, 23, 39,
    43, 45, 46, 50
US 1st Cavalry Division 20
US 101st Airborne **33**
US 25th Infantry Division **22**
US Airborne Division 32, **32**
US air cavalry **21**
US airlift 47
US Army 25, 28
US bombing of North Vietnam 16
US casualties in Vietnam 13
US Congress **14, 15**, 37, 45
US embassy 28, 29, 47
US fighter aircraft **16**
US helicopter pilots **10**
US Marines **18**, 19, **25, 26, 26**, 27,
    30, 35, 38
US military advisers **12**
US military commitment in
    Vietnam 1965-8 **19**, 25
US military personnel in 1969-71
    19, **34**
US Navy 25
US servicemen killed in Vietnam

25
US Special Forces **12**, 13
US troops 25, **26**
US warships 42
US withdrawal from Vietnam 32,
    44

Van Tien Dung, General *see* Dung,
    General Van Tien
Viet Cong (VC) 11, 12, 13, 18, 19,
    20, 22, 23, **24**, 25, 26, 27, 28
    bases 25
    guerrillas **20, 23**
Viet Minh 5, 6, 7, **7**, 8, 9, 11
    artillery **8**
    guerrillas **6, 7**
    territory held by in 1954 **7 map**
Vietnam 4, 5, 6, **7**, 8, **8**, 19, **49**
    army of (ARVN) 10, 11, 12, **12**,
    13
    China's border war with in 1979
    50
    Chinese invasion of **49 map**, 50
    Democratic Republic of 9, **9**,
    division of in 1954 9, **9 map**
    Doc Lap Dong Minh Ho (League
    for the Independence of
    Vietnam) 4
    independence of 5
    Republic of 9, **9**
    Socialist Republic of 48
    under French rule **7 map**
Vietnamese soldiers **7**
Vietnamese Workers' Party 9
Vietnamization 32, 37
Vo Nguyen Giap *see* Giap, Vo
    Nguyen
Vu Gia River **35**

War Powers Resolution 45
Watergate affair 45
Westmoreland, General William C.
    15, 19, 20, 21, **27**, 30, 31, 33, 54
World War II 4, 5

X-ray landing zone **20**
Xuan Loc **46**, 47

Zais, General Melvin 32